Prioritize, Organize

The Art of Getting It Done

By Peg Pickering

National Press Publications

A Division of Rockhurst University Continuing Education Center, Inc.
6901 West 63rd St. • P.O. Box 2949 • Shawnee Mission, KS 66201-1349
1-800-258-7246 • 1-913-432-7757

**Prioritize, Organize —
The Art of Getting It Done**

Copyright 1999, National Press Publications

      A Division of Rockhurst University Continuing Education Center, Inc.

Printed in the United States of America

 2 3 4 5 6 7 8 9 10

ISBN 1-55852-246-8

About Rockhurst University Continuing Education Center, Inc.

Rockhurst University Continuing Education Center, Inc., is committed to providing lifelong learning opportunities through the integration of innovative education and training.

National Seminars Group, a division of Rockhurst University Continuing Education Center, Inc., has its finger on the pulse of America's business community. We've trained more than 2 million people in every imaginable occupation to be more productive and advance their careers. Along the way, we've learned a few things. What it takes to be successful ... how to build the skills to make it happen ... and how to translate learning into results. Millions of people from thousands of companies around the world turn to National Seminars for training solutions.

National Press Publications is our product and publishing division. We offer a complete line of the finest self-study and continuous-learning resources available anywhere. These products present our industry-acclaimed curriculum and training expertise in a concise, action-oriented format you can put to work right away. Packed with real-world strategies and hands-on techniques, these resources are guaranteed to help you meet the career and personal challenges you face every day.

Legend Symbol Guide

 Exercises that reinforce your learning experience

 Questions that will help you apply the critical points to your situation

 Checklists that will help you identify important issues for future application

 Key issues to learn and understand for future application

C
A
S
E

S
T
U
D
Y

Real-world case studies that will help you apply the information you've learned

Table of Contents

FOREWORD

Frustrated by an inability to make decisions because of the seeming importance of everything awaiting you? Do many days begin with a feeling of being overwhelmed by the projects and activities on your daily list all crying for attention at the same time? Can you keep up with the development of new software designed to simplify your life? Do you sometimes look back after an exhausting day and wonder what was accomplished and why moving at breakneck speed was required? Tired of sacrificing your personal priorities for the job?

Overworked. Overwhelmed. Frustrated. Stressed out. That about sums it up for most people. The pace of business ... and life ... has and will continue to accelerate exponentially. Not too many years ago, the advent of Federal Express overnight delivery was a phenomenal innovation. Everyday usage of the fax, the proliferation of voice mail, the explosion of computer usage, e-mail and the Internet have radically altered the pace of business forever.

In the 1970s, good time management was key to success. The 1980s required excellent time management, the ability to deal with paper proliferation and a rudimentary level of computer knowledge. Success in the 1990s required outstanding time management, powerful mechanisms to minimize paperwork and a fair degree of computer savvy. The millennium requires not only superb time and paper management, outstanding computer skills and communication skills but also the ability to cope with the increasing frenetic pace of technological innovation and the ongoing avalanche of information.

So much is transpiring so fast that no one can keep pace. No one.

As a result, choices must be made. Priorities must be set. Personal productivity and self-management skills must be sharpened. Conflicting priorities and expectations must be juggled. Stress must be controlled. A new sense of balance is needed. The very essence of how we work and live must change.

It is no longer true that "if you do what you've always done, you'll get what you've always gotten." Today, if you do what you've always done, you'll simply get further and further behind. More and more pressured. More and more stressed. In short, organizing is not optional. It is mandatory.

> *THE FIRST LAW OF ORGANIZATION:*
> *CHANGE ... OR DIE!*

*I*NTRODUCTION

If you've bought any kind of sophisticated electronic equipment recently — anything from a personal computer to a video recorder — that equipment came with a user's manual: A "how-to" publication acquainting you with what you bought, showing you how to install it and use it to your advantage. As the result of the information you gained through the self-study opportunity provided by the user's manual, your effectiveness in using what you already had was greatly increased, as was your satisfaction.

The manual you have in your hands is a user's manual for each of the 24 hours of every day. Use it for that list of things to do that seems to grow instead of shrink and that never is completed. Use it to manage the people who attempt to control and change events in your life through the new demands and challenges to your already full schedule. Use it whenever you feel competing priorities call for you to make a decision as to what to do and when it should be done. Use it to bring balance to your life.

This self-study user's manual contains practical information you can use in your daily business activities and in your personal life as well. It also serves as a guide to developing the thought processes essential to creating and fulfilling a personally effective strategy. Assimilation of the ideas and concepts will be quick and easy.

After reading the manual, you will be able to analyze yourself more effectively and work more productively, whether you're the owner of your own business, a manager or supervisor, or a support team member vital to your organization's success. This book is not something to be read once and put aside. It's full of material that can be reviewed and processed regularly, because true command of principles and ideas comes only with regular, conscientious application.

These principles and ideas are fundamental to successful application of the Strategic Organizing and Managing Process.

Strategic Organizing & Managing Process

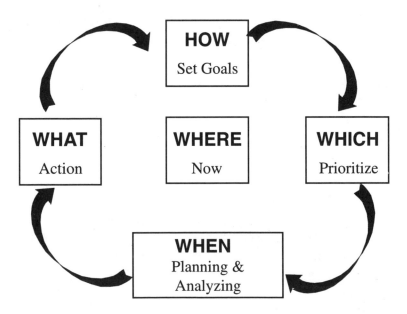

The WHERE in the center is where you are right now. In order to begin any strategic process, the first requirement is to know the starting point. Once that has been determined, the following four components must be evaluated.

- HOW you organize and manage your life is developed by your goal-setting system.

- WHICH goals you live by are identified by your priorities.

- WHEN you reach your goals is determined by your planning.

- Life is the WHAT — the action steps you must take to fulfill your plans and achieve the goals you've set based on your priorities.

The result of living out your plans brings you full circle as you continually reconsider the goals you set. And so the process begins again. This book will enable you to apply this process to every aspect of your life … allowing you to work more effectively, to become more personally fulfilled … and to be radically less stressed!

"If one advances confidently in the direction of his dreams, and endeavors to live the life which he has imagined, he will meet with a success unexpected in the common hours."

—Thoreau

*C*HAPTER 1

Self-Management: Key to Balance

"If you want things to be different, perhaps the answer is to become different yourself."

Norman Vincent Peale

"So much work, so little time."

"There just isn't enough time to get it all done."

"No matter how many hours I put in, I just never get caught up."

Sound familiar? Most people today feel swamped, overworked, and overwhelmed with the demands on their time. To regain control and lower the stress level, one must internalize some fundamental truths before embarking on a recovery plan.

> *Fact:*
> *TO CONTROL YOUR LIFE,*
> *YOU MUST CONTROL YOUR TIME.*

"To waste your time is to waste your life, but to master your time is to master your life and make the most of it."

Alan Laiken

> *Fact:*
> *WE ALL HAVE ALL THE TIME THERE IS.*

Lamenting the lack of time is a futile endeavor — a complete waste of time and energy. Everyone has 24 hours in a day. Precisely 1440 minutes. That's it. No more, no less. You may wish you had more time than you do, but it's just not possible. This is one of the few ways in which all people are equal. You must make do with what you have.

Where does the time go? Those who accomplish the most know precisely where each minute is spent. Identifying time wasters and personal inefficiencies is critical to success in our fast-paced world.

> *Fact:*
> *YOU CANNOT SAVE TIME —*
> *YOU CAN ONLY SPEND IT OR INVEST IT.*

The concept of time is well represented by the hourglass. The sand passes through constantly, at the same rate. You can't stick your finger in and stop it. In the last minute each one of us has spent 60 seconds of time that can never be retrieved.

The great Finnish runner Paavo Nurmi set and then lowered several times the world record for the mile run in the 1920s. On one such occasion, a college student who had just learned of the accomplishment exclaimed to one of his professors, "Dr. Rogers, Paavo Nurmi has broken the world record for the mile by two seconds. Two whole seconds!"

His professor looked at him for a moment and replied, "And what does Mr. Nurmi intend to do with the time he saved?"

The bad news, then, is that you simply can't save time. But there's good news as well. You can spend your time wisely by investing it in ways that will give you future payoffs in productivity and freedom in decision-making. Which activities can you invest time in now to give you the greatest Return on Time Invested (ROTI)?

> *Fact:*
> **PUTTING IN MORE HOURS IS NOT THE ANSWER.**

The longer you work, the *less* you will accomplish ... and the more likely you will be to undo everything you've done. Most people accept this fact in theory, but often don't acknowledge it in practice. The old advice holds true: "Don't confuse activity with accomplishment." The computer has driven this idea deep into our minds. Did you ever delete the last hour's worth of input with one tired, fatal mistake?

If you insist on working yourself past reasonable limits, you are not only inviting major imbalance into your life, you also allow the Law of Diminishing Returns, closely followed by the Law of Counterproductivity, to take over.

The answer lies in the *efficient and effective use* of one's 1440 minutes each day. Being busy must be changed to being productive. *Time management and organization skills are not the problem. Self-management skills are.*

Assessment: Self-Management Profile

Answer these questions with yes or no. Absolute candor with yourself is essential.

_____ 1. I do what I like before I do what I don't like.

_____ 2. I do the things I know how to do faster than the things I don't know how to do.

_____ 3. I do the things that are easiest before doing things that are hard.

_____ 4. I tackle small jobs before I tackle large jobs.

_____ 5. I do things for which the resources are readily available.

_____ 6. I sometimes do unscheduled things before I do scheduled things.

_____ 7. I respond to demands from others before I respond to demands from myself.

_____ 8. I do things that are urgent before I do things that are important.

_____ 9. I readily respond to crises and emergencies.

_____ 10. I do interesting things before I do uninteresting things.

_____ 11. I do things that are politically expedient.

_____ 12. I do things that provide the most closure.

_____ 13. I respond on the basis of who wants it.

_____ 14. I work on things in the order of their arrival.

_____ 15. I work on the squeaky wheel principle.

The more yes answers you have, the more habits you must eliminate to more effectively manage yourself, your time, your productivity ... and your stress level.

You are the complex product of many experiences accumulated and blended over your lifetime. Changing your long-standing habits will require willingness to evaluate your existing methods and attitudes, to learn new approaches, and to develop new habits to replace the ineffective ones. Make a firm commitment to and strong, consistent implementation of each successive step in the change process.

HABIT

I am your constant companion.
I am your greatest helper or your heaviest burden.
I will push you onward or drag you down to failure.
I am completely at your command.

Half the things you do, you might just as well turn over to me,
And I will be able to do them quickly and correctly.
I am easily managed; you must merely be firm with me.
Show me exactly how you want something done,
And after a few lessons I will do it automatically.

I am the servant of all great men
And, alas, of all failures as well.
Those who are great, I have made great.
Those of you who are failures, I have made failures.

I am not a machine, though I work with all the precision of a machine
Plus the intelligence of a man.
You may run me for profit, or run me for ruin
It makes no difference to me.

Take me, train me, be firm with me
And I will put the world at your feet.
Be easy with me, and I will destroy you.
Who am I?

I am HABIT!

Author Unknown

In short, changing your old habits will take time, effort and focused attention. There are no magic answers. Change will not occur spontaneously. Your existing habits were not developed overnight; and it is unrealistic to expect a quick fix to provide permanent replacements for them.

Your habits are the cords tying the pieces of your life together. A new habit is like a thin string ... weak, vulnerable. As a habit becomes more and more ingrained over time, that string turns into thick, braided rope capable of supporting a great deal of weight ... and requiring a great deal of effort to move it. That's fantastic ... if that habit is a good one. Not so good if the habit leaves a lot to be desired.

Replacing an old habit with a new one is like trying to replace that thick braided rope with a delicate, new string. The new string can't take over immediately. It's not strong enough or firmly enough in place. There must be a transition period where the new and the old coexist. As you *actively work* to strengthen the new habit, the old one will begin to weaken and fall away. *But only if you remain focused on strengthening the new one.*

Fortunately, the process of acquiring new habits doesn't take forever. William James, the "Father of Modern Psychology," noted that it takes from 21 to 30 days of consistent, spaced repetition of an activity to eliminate an old habit or to develop a new one. Constant improvement, not perfection, should be your goal. Improvement means finding solutions to problems. The result is not only increased productivity but also a feeling of accomplishment and a boost to morale that leads to further improvement.

The key here is commitment. You must truly be committed to regain control ... to reestablishing your priorities and balance in your life ... to do the work necessary to change your habits. Are you?

Self-Management Solutions: An Overview

High achievers have high energy levels and are highly motivated because of some personal focus or need they are trying to fulfill. What's yours? Clarity of purpose fuels motivation to create new skills and new tools to obtain higher levels of productivity. All improvements can be traced to the enhancement of one or more of the following areas.

- **Clearly Defined Mission/Goals.** Without a specific sense of purpose, it's impossible to effectively manage and organize your priorities. Where are you going? What is your purpose in life? Why did you show up for work today? What is your department's specific purpose for existence? Do you have an organizational mission statement, and do you know it off the top of your head?

  In Chapter 3 you'll find valuable tools to help you determine both personal and business mission statements and to establish clear, focused goals to keep your life and business moving in your desired direction.

- **Establishing and Communicating Priorities.** The best daily action list ever written is useless and ineffective if the relative importance of each item on the list hasn't been established. It's easy to fall into a trap of getting many things completed, but doing the wrong things. Rather than doing the most important items first, people sometimes work on things that are easiest to accomplish, more fun, or closer at hand.

  You must know what's really important to you and your organization to make decisions that will make effective use of your time. The organizational tools in Chapter 5 are invaluable in determining what's really important and provide a logical sequence to get things done. Chapter 9 focuses on communicating these priorities to keep other people's efforts in sync with your own.

- **Daily Action Plan.** Beginning your day without a plan of action is a formula for spending all day doing the wrong things. It invites anyone and everyone to interrupt your activities with their requests and assignments. You will passively allow unwelcome intrusions, because you'll have no way to defend yourself. Chapters 4 and 9 respectively describe how effective your defense can be through prior planning and good communication.

- **Saying "NO" to Overcommitment.** For many, there's not a lot wrong with the way in which projects are planned, tackled and completed. It's the sheer number of projects taken on that becomes overwhelming. (If you're thinking "that's me!" — you're right.) You must learn to say "NO" and mean it. Chapter 6 tells you how.

- **Focus on Finishing — Not on Perfection.** Are you unable to complete and release a project until it is done perfectly? Can you still see ways for something to be done better? Even if you can't see anything, does it nag you that there must be something you've overlooked? How much time and energy do you waste pursuing the impossible dream, perfectionism? Perfectionism can be controlled with the ideas and techniques contained in Chapter 7.

- **Paper Control and Workspace Organization.** No matter how well organized your priorities are or how effective your daily plan, you may be losing valuable, irretrievable time searching for things that are lost in the mess on your desk, in your files, drawers, closets and even in your car. Chapter 7 can make all the difference.

- **Decisiveness.** The decision-making process is only as good as the planning preceding it. Without adequate planning and prioritizing, there's always the risk of rushing into catastrophe or watching opportunity disappear from a failure to respond with any action at all. Chapter 4 deals with planning; Chapter 7 will aid you in confident, effective decision-making.

- **Calm Crisis Management.** Life is extremely frustrating when we're caught in the constant search for extinguishers to put out the fires that break out day after day. Productivity can be put on hold, indefinitely, as neglected situations suddenly become urgent. You can't prevent fires if you spend all your time putting them out!

  One of the greatest benefits of the kind of planning discussed in Chapter 4 is the elimination of many crises from daily activities. When a crisis is unavoidable, as it sometimes is, the steps in Chapter 11 describe a sure-fire method to get you through.

- **Effective Delegation.** Without a doubt, the "I can do it better myself" philosophy has created more career burnout and lost opportunity than any other single factor. Failure to communicate effectively when delegating probably ranks number two. In Chapter 9 you'll discover a highly effective way to get other people committed to your plans through confident delegation.

- **Controlling Interruptions.** Your day can be going according to schedule, and then the telephone rings or an unexpected visitor drops in and productivity instantly wanes. Many of these occurrences can be eliminated; those that can't be eliminated must be controlled. If this is a problem for you, you'll find solutions in Chapter 8.

- **Monitoring Projects/Deadlines.** Have you ever looked up one day and realized your most important project's deadline was three days away ... and you still had three more weeks of work to complete? Heard people talking about their flow charts but have no idea how to make one work for you? Chapter 10 is what you need.

- **Effective Meetings.** Meetings are the only place where "minutes are kept and hours are wasted." Unplanned, unnecessary meetings involving the wrong people waste millions of hours and billions of dollars each year. Often, those that are planned and necessary are ineffective because of poor preparation or follow-up. Effective meeting planning, as described in Chapter 9, is the key to making these times useful and productive.

- **Eliminating Procrastination.** The universal tendency to put off until tomorrow what should be done today is a major productivity killer at work and home. All too often people immerse themselves in unimportant activities while the really important work remains undone. If you're ready to tackle this issue now, turn to Chapter 7.

- **Life Balance and Stress Reduction.** The ultimate goal for most people. As outside pressures build, as the pace of the work becomes more and more frenetic, your ability to make good choices ... to establish balance in your life ... and manage your stress level is essential for survival. If the pace of your life and the demands on your time are getting to be too much for you, read Chapter 12. Make each day a joy rather than a burden.

Becoming proficient in each of these areas is critical to a self-management/productivity improvement plan. New habits of effectiveness and efficiency must be acquired little by little, step by step over time. Change is essential for survival. Everyone knows that, yet many continue to do the same old things while giving lip service to the need for change.

Much of the stress people feel comes from not keeping agreements they've made with themselves. They promise they're going to get organized and then don't. They start a multitude of projects and finish only two. Self-management is about closing the gap between what you say and what you do. Productivity is about completion. Both require a commitment to action and follow-through. Remember:

It doesn't matter what you start ... All that matters is what you finish!

Make a Commitment to Your Commitment

Have you ever charged into a new project determined to make a change ... then hit an obstacle? Shrugged your shoulders, said "Well, that didn't work," and gone back to the old, comfortable approach?

Did you really give the new process a fair trial? Most likely not. Just because you stumbled is no reason to give up! What would you say to your child if he were in that situation? Something like, "If at first you don't succeed, try, try again"? So why did you say, "Since at first I didn't succeed, I'll just quit"?

Or maybe you thought, "That's a good idea but it won't work." Think about the logic of that. If it won't work, it's not a good idea ... it's a fantasy.

> *Fact:*
> ## IF IT REALLY IS A GOOD IDEA, THERE'S A WAY TO MAKE IT WORK.

Keep at it. Tweak it. Modify it to fit your situation or circumstances.

Trying something new is disconcerting. It's also normal. But you want to do it well. You want to do it right. You want to do it NOW. Keep in mind what Zig Ziglar says.

"Anything worth doing right is worth doing badly until you can learn to do it right."

Keep going. Keep trying. Most good ideas are uncomfortable at first.

This book is full of good ideas. Many of them will require you to do things differently. Many may seem difficult. You'll make some false starts and backslide periodically. That's normal. It's all part of the learning and change process. Just keep your commitment to your commitment and keep going. And remember:

To reach any significant goal, you must leave your comfort zone!

Ten Tips for a Fast Start

Keeping yourself motivated along the road to organization is not an easy task. Permanent change takes time and motivation is hard to maintain while waiting to see results. That's why it is critical to get off to a fast start and to do things from which you see and feel immediate results. You need that sense of accomplishment and the feeling that the effort really is paying off. You periodically need a quick motivation fix.

After all, isn't that why you cross those items off your "to do" list at the end of the day? Crossing off those items gives you that needed feeling of progress ... and helps to motivate you to continue with the other items on the list. Have you ever reviewed that list at the end of the day and realized you did a number of things that were not on the list ... so you wrote them down just so you could cross them off? That's the feeling of accomplishment you need to continue on the road to permanent change.

Here is a list of things you can do *immediately* to "jump-start" your organizational improvement process. More detailed explanations and rationales for these items follow throughout the text of this manual.

1. **Start by doing a complete "mind-dump."** Make a set of master lists of all the incomplete items running around in your brain ... large and small. Time and energy are wasted trying to mentally keep up with it all. For the mind-dump list to be effective, it must be complete. Take whatever time it takes.

    *   Projects List — all ongoing
    *   Next Actions List — itemizes next step(s) to be taken on all active projects
    *   Waiting List — records all items that must come from someone else
    *   Calendar — time and day specific actions
    *   Someday/Maybe List — all discretionary tasks

    As additional items come to mind later, jot them onto the lists. Do not worry about prioritizing. All you're trying to accomplish here is some mental breathing room. If the pending item is recorded on the mind-dump lists, you can stop worrying about it until it is time to work on it.

2. **Set up a tickler file today.**

3. **Clear your desk completely.** Quickly look at each item. Don't read every word ... you'll never finish. Some astute person once said, "Anyone who can read is never successful at cleaning up the office." Avoid that trap.

   - If it is an action item, decide on what date you will act, note it in the upper right-hand corner and file in the tickler file.

   - If it is to be filed, put it in a "to be filed" bin. (Not on your desk or in your in-box.)

   - If it should be on someone else's desk, send it there.

   - If in doubt, throw it out.

4. **Separate reference from reading.** Chances are you will not get around to reading all the professional journals, etc. File away the ones you need to keep for future reference and place only those with immediate applicability in your reading file.

5. **Move your in-box off your desk, out of your line of sight, preferably outside the door of your office.**

6. **Institute the two-minute rule.** Anytime you are confronted with an action item that will take less than two minutes, do it immediately.

7. **Stand up whenever you talk on the phone.**

8. **Do the most important item first thing each morning.**

9. **Identify your peak productivity time and protect it from interruptions.**

10. **Realign your stress level.** Use these common sense tips for keeping your adrenaline levels from maxing out.

- Look out the window. People who sit near a window have 23% fewer complaints of headache, backache and exhaustion.

- Exercise outside. Studies show that those who exercise indoors are less likely to keep it up.

- Lighten up your workout. There is no consistent relationship between the intensity of the workout and the mental health benefit.

- Relax after your workout. Lie down, close your eyes, float. The endorphins released in your workout keep you in an alpha state for about 20 minutes. When you get up and return to your normal activities, you'll move into a beta-wave state — invigorated and ready to tackle whatever is next.

- Change your mindset. Dwelling on problems, especially those you cannot control, does nothing but increase your stress level. Accept the things you cannot change and move on. Laugh at the absurdities of life.

That should get you started. These fast-start suggestions, however, will not be enough by themselves to get everything under control ... but they will give you an immediate focus for improvement while you are studying the details throughout this manual.

"Many of us spend half of our time wishing for things we could have if we didn't spend half of our time wishing."

Alexander Woolcott

Summary of Key Points

- If you want to manage and organize your priorities, you must first learn to manage yourself.

- Recognize and accept areas you can't control; note areas you can control and act upon them.

- You already have as much time as there is, and there isn't any more.

- You can't save time, you can only spend it. Spend it where it will give you the greatest returns.

- Working too long can actually reduce or erase your productivity.

- If you work smarter, instead of harder, you can be productive and relaxed at the same time.

- Look for your personal application of every idea in this manual.

- Successful self-management is the result of developing good habits and letting them control you, thereby giving you freedom.

- It takes 30 days of conscious, spaced repetition of an action to develop a new habit or eliminate an old one.

- If things aren't getting done, there are many common productivity killers that may be at fault.

- Recognize your weaknesses and develop a plan to build new habits there.

- New habits are fragile. Creating them requires commitment.

Putting Self-Management Solutions to Work in Your Life

1. How can you best manage and organize the priorities of your life?

2. To develop a new habit, what should you do? How long should it take?

3. What three rules apply to developing new habits?

4. When are you going to start? Have you made a commitment to your commitment?

5. Chart a 30-day course of action. Reassess your progress in 30 days and modify your plan.

Action TNT — Today Not Tomorrow

No one ever built a reputation based on what they were going to do tomorrow.

MY IDEAS
ABOUT SELF-MANAGEMENT:

CHAPTER 2

Fundamental Organizational Principles

"It is more than probable that the average man could, with no injury to his health, increase his efficiency fifty percent."

Walter Dill Scott

Principle #1:
The Slight Edge Principle

Write it down any place you'll see it frequently. Make this law so much a part of you it becomes an automatic part of your thought process and, therefore, your actions. Use it to understand fully the infinitesimal difference between success and failure, between productivity and frustration, between happiness and agony.

> *SMALL CHANGES, OVER TIME, MAKE A BIG DIFFERENCE.*

That's it. Simple yet profoundly powerful. An illustration from horseracing can illustrate the truth of this simple little idea.

In racing's Triple Crown series for three-year-olds, there is a $5 million bonus to any horse that can win all three races: The Kentucky Derby, The Preakness and The Belmont Stakes. Should one horse fail to win all three races, there is still a $1 million bonus for the horse with the best overall record in the three races.

During the 1989 series, two horses, Sunday Silence and Easy Goer, were clearly the best of the field. Sunday Silence easily won The Kentucky Derby, Easy Goer was just as dominant in The Belmont. In each race the other horse finished second. The difference, as it turned out, was the middle race — The Preakness.

In this race the two horses staged a thrilling run down the stretch to the finish line, way ahead of the other horses. In a photo finish, Sunday Silence won the race (and subsequently the bonus) by a nose. First place in the race was worth about $700,000, plus the million dollar bonus for a total of $1,700,000. Second place was worth $70,000.

Sunday Silence got about 25 times more money for his efforts than did Easy Goer! Was Sunday Silence 25 times better than Easy Goer? Hardly. Over three races covering five weeks and nearly four miles of running, one horse was about two inches better than the other. There was virtually no difference, but the payoff was 25 times greater!

That's what the Slight Edge Principle is all about. Little changes, over time. Maybe just a little more training. Maybe a slightly better method of planning. Maybe just one tiny habit overcome. Maybe all of those and more. Each one is almost inconsequential, but when added up, the advantage is incredible!

That's really the major promise of this manual. If you can identify these little advantages and have patience and persistence to carry them through, the payoff will be exponential!

You certainly don't have to work harder. Smarter is achieved in a number of small steps, one at a time. Most people attempt to free up large chunks of time when they embark on a time management improvement and give up, frustrated, when they are unsuccessful. It is much easier, more productive, and less frustrating to concentrate on the little changes and then look at their cumulative effect.

The Slight Edge Principle is the reason that, at the end of each chapter of this book, you have a chance to take time to reflect on the ideas discussed. Sort them through and identify the key ideas that you can apply to your situation to make The Law of the Slight Edge work in your favor. Write those ideas down in the space provided at the end of each chapter.

Principle #2:
The 80-20 Rule (Pareto Principle)

Another rule that you can apply to make a difference in how well you organize and manage your priorities is the Pareto Principle, also known as the "80-20 Rule."

Victor Pareto was an Italian economist and sociologist at the turn of the 20th century who studied the ownership of land in Italy. Pareto discovered that more than 80 percent of all the land was actually owned by less than 20 percent of the people. As he studied other things that people owned (including money), he found the same principle held true: 20 percent or less of the people always ended up with 80 percent or more of whatever he measured.

This law is so well accepted by economists that most agree that if all the world's assets could be evenly distributed to every person in the world, it would only be a matter of time (and a short one, at that) until 20 percent of the people had 80 percent of the assets all over again.

This book isn't about economics; however, the principle has proven to hold just as true concerning such issues as time management and productivity on the job.

Do you work in sales? Less than 20 percent of sales people typically produce more than 80 percent of a company's sales. Are you a manager? Twenty percent of your people probably cause 80 percent of the problems you have to deal with and require 80 percent of the total time you spend with all your people.

Are you a volunteer worker? Then you probably agree that less than 20 percent of the people do 80 percent or more of all the work that gets done.

Do you work with many people on your job? Does at least 80 percent of the benefit come from only 20 percent of those people? Who are these productive people? Identify them, and decisions about priorities are already made!

Look at your list of projects and activities. About 20 percent of those priorities are producing 80 percent of the results coming from your work. And in many cases, the first 20 percent of the time you spend working on a job will produce 80 percent of the payoff you get.

The most astonishing revelation about the 80-20 Rule is its opposite side: If 20 percent of activities are producing 80 percent of the results, then the other 80 percent of activities are, in total, only giving 20 percent of the results. What a waste of time and energy!

Perfectionism is frequently the biggest stumbling block to accomplishment when we reach this point. Is the last 10 percent really worth it? In some cases it is, but not usually. Time-management expert Alec Mackenzie writes: "I practiced the art of getting more things done, rather than getting the really important things done well."

Getting things done is the name of the game. The more you get done, the greater your productivity. Yet some of us cling to a few "really important" priorities, trying to do them just a little better. You must learn to ask yourself: Is it already good enough? Is it necessary to put any more time and effort into this project? Would my time and effort be better spent elsewhere?

What activities will produce the greatest Return on Time Invested for you? When you can identify them, you can focus your energy for maximum benefit.

Most people acknowledge the truth of the 80-20 Rule without having a true picture of what it means. Does it mean one person (or one project) will have or produce four times as much? No, it's not nearly that conservative.

Picture five people sitting down at a table to eat a pie cut in five equal pieces. If this pie is apportioned to these people according to the 80-20 Rule, one person will end up with four of the five pieces of pie and the other four will have to share the remaining piece. The benefit to the one is 16 times greater than to any one of the other four people. Four people get five percent each while the fifth person gets 80 percent!

Remember: To apply the 80-20 Rule to managing your priorities, remind yourself that 20 percent of the activities on your list are going to produce 80 percent of the results and payoff. Your question must constantly be, "Which activities are the 20-percenters?"

Principle #3: The Bowling Ball Principle ("In-Between" Time)

Envision your day as a box. Each major project/task/priority is a bowling ball. They are very large, heavy, and require a great deal of space. Not a single additional bowling ball will fit into your box ... but a great number of marbles can be sprinkled in the small empty spaces around the balls. You simply cannot take on an additional major responsibility ... but you can accomplish all those little, annoying but critical small tasks by utilizing the "In-Between" time.

You can make your days more productive and satisfying by identifying the little windows of opportunity that pass through your life each day. They don't arrive with much fanfare, so if you're not alert to them, they will sneak right past you. These snippets of minutes are called "In-Between" time.

Did you ever call someone on the phone and promptly get put on hold? Ever have a 10:00 meeting that really didn't get started until 10:15? Ever finish up a major activity just before lunch? Ever sit in a lobby or waiting room for your appointment?

	Cumulative Effects of Wasted Minutes		
Minutes per day	**Minutes per week**	**Hours per year**	**8-hour days per year**
5	35	30	3.8
10	70	60	7.6
15	105	90	11.4
30	140	120	15.8
60	280	340	31.6

Each of these five- and 10-minute periods may seem insignificant, but taken together they can form a powerful force of accomplishment. How much in-between time do you have in a day? Ten minutes? Twenty? Thirty? If you lose those 30 minutes every day, by the end of the year you will have lost 15.8 eight-hour days!! That's over three work weeks! Would you feel more in control of your life with an added two weeks work time each year, at no cost to your vacation schedule or normal working hours? Would this increase your value to your organization?

To recapture control of your in-between time, you must plan for it and be prepared when it presents itself.

> ## *IF YOU DON'T HAVE A PLAN, YOU WILL WASTE THIS TIME!*

> ## *Fact:*
> ## *CONSISTENT PLANNING LEVERAGES TIME AND INCREASES FOCUS.*

The best time to develop a plan of action is ... NOW! What are some small activities, without specific deadlines, that could fit into this time? Here are some suggestions.

- Return phone calls.
- Sign letters that have been typed and are ready to mail.
- Keep a reading file at your desk, and read something.
- Clean up your desk and return things to their proper places.
- Review your daily action list and reprioritize, if necessary.
- Update your waiting and next actions lists.
- Go through your mail.
- Write a quick note or memo.
- Relax! Catch your breath!

The problem is that many people fritter time away and then feel guilty when it's gone. Make a conscious decision to do one of these things (including relaxation) and this time will hardly ever be wasted. Have a plan!

Is making the most of even small periods of time worth it? Remember, *small things over time make a big difference*!

Making It Work

CONCERN	REASON	STRATEGY
not enough time	belief there's more time out there somewhere	use what you have—there isn't any more
how can I save time?	thinking time can be saved	spend it wisely, because you can't save it at all
I need to work longer	if I do, I can get more done	don't confuse activity with accomplishment
I need to work harder	that's how to be productive	work smarter—relax, and keep in control that way
I need to make major changes in my style	I want to improve	apply small changes over time—use the slight edge
too many projects, too many people	all must be treated equally	learn the 80-20 rule: valued few or trivial many?
no time for small demands	can't schedule them in	don't schedule: have ready for "In-Between" times

Fact:
IF YOU SPEND MINUTES WISELY, THE HOURS AND DAYS TAKE CARE OF THEMSELVES.

Summary of Key Points

- Commit to memory The Law of the Slight Edge: Small changes, over time, make a big difference!

- Apply the 80-20 Rule to your people and projects: Focus on the valued few, not the trivial many, and learn to recognize each.

- You probably can't put any more large projects into your day, but there are lots of little ones you can do if you use in-between time.

- Always have small projects ready to work on as soon as you notice that in-between time is occurring.

- Five extra minutes, three times a day, equals almost two additional weeks of productive time during a year.

Putting Organizational Principles to Work in Your Life

1. What is the Slight Edge Principle? Have you written some Slight-Edge ideas at the end of the chapter yet? Be sure to list at least five.

2. How, specifically, can you put the 80-20 Rule to work in your life to make a difference in productivity and accomplishment? Which activities are your 20 percenters? Which items are taking too much of your time for too little return?

3. List three in-between times you have on a regular basis. What do you now plan to do with each of those times?

2

4. Prioritize your choices from the first three questions and commit to an action plan to put them to work.

5. Chart a 30-day course of action. Reassess your progress in 30 days and modify your plan.

Action TNT — Today Not Tomorrow

No one ever built a reputation based on what they were going to do tomorrow.

MY SLIGHT-EDGE IDEAS
ABOUT ORGANIZATIONAL PRINCIPLES:

2

CHAPTER 3

Planning With a Mission

"Long range planning does not deal with future decisions, but with the future of present decisions."

Peter Drucker

Before you can begin the process of day-to-day planning, you must look at the big picture. You cannot possibly develop a workable plan and establish logical and accurate priorities without knowing what the end goal is. Many people try, and their lack of results reflects it. The big picture is essential to determining your priorities.

3

Assessment: Examining Your Goal Orientation

After reading each of the following statements, circle your response.

	Agree	Unsure	Disagree
1. My organization has a mission statement.	3	2	1
2. I know my organization's mission statement.	3	2	1
3. I agree with that mission statement.	3	2	1
4. I have a personal mission statement to guide my decisions.	3	2	1
5. I have specific, written goals for my job.	3	2	1
6. I have specific, written goals for my career.	3	2	1
7. I have specific, written goals for my personal life.	3	2	1
8. My job, career and personal goals are mutually compatible.	3	2	1
9. If a challenge arose today, I know people who would help me.	3	2	1

Interpretation:

22 or more:	You know where you're going, and you're getting there!
21-14:	With a little more work, you'll be all right.
Less than 14:	You need to explore what things are important to you and learn to set goals.

The Mission Statement: The First and Last Step

If you were to approach your boss today and ask, "What are we doing here?" or, "We opened our doors for business today. Why?" — what do you suppose would happen? Would your boss smile and begin to explain quite clearly the answers? Or would you get that puzzled expression that can only mean "You're obviously not playing with a full deck"?

You probably know which reaction you would get. But do you know the answers to the questions asked? Most people and, indeed, most organizations, don't know. That's why there are so many organizations floating in a sea of confusion. In many cases, this problem has moved past the humorous to the critical.

Determining the ultimate meaning and purpose of life are as necessary to personal and corporate survival as air, food or water is to physical existence. Consequently, a mission statement is something every individual and every organization ought to have because it is a *reason for existence*.

When the reason for existence is known, understood, accepted and communicated, things happen in a big way. Without it, energy and effort are wasted; and an organization can't last long going around in circles.

3

A mission statement should fit three qualifications, whether it's a personal or organizational statement. The mission statement must be:

- Distinct. It should be yours, and no one else's.

- Stimulating. It should stir you to action on its behalf.

- Motivating. It should inspire and excite you.

The mission statement is a somewhat short but specific statement that clearly identifies the major purposes of the organization that must be foremost in the minds of all employees at all times.

Examples:

Johnson & Johnson

Part of Johnson & Johnson's mission statement reads:

OUR #1 COMMITMENT IS TO THE DOCTORS, NURSES, PATIENTS AND FAMILIES WHO RELY ON OUR PRODUCTS.

A mission statement not only guides in times of prosperity and success, it also provides leadership in crisis. When a package of Tylenol® manufactured by Johnson & Johnson was tampered with and contaminated, the mission statement was critical. During this crisis, it immediately advised employees what to do. The first thing the company did when the tainted bottles were discovered was to pull all of the product from the shelves.

A bold move? Yes. Expensive? Definitely. But it was the only move that made sense, considering the commitment expressed in the mission statement. Nothing is more important to a pharmaceuticals company than public trust; and Johnson & Johnson's mission statement reflected this fact. Today, Johnson & Johnson still rates at the top of every survey of public trust and confidence in the product. Johnson & Johnson survived a crisis that might have killed many other companies and came back to achieve higher trust levels than ever before.

By the way, who do you suppose made the decision to take all the Tylenol® off the shelves? The Chief Executive Officer? The Chairman of the Board? Actually, a relatively low-level executive happened to be the first to learn of the problem and made the call. With the confidence only a clear, purposeful mission statement can provide, the decision was made immediately at that level.

Rockhurst University Continuing Education Center (National Seminars, Inc.)

Of all the many public seminar providers nationwide, National Seminars truly stands alone at the forefront because of the simplicity and clarity of its purpose.

QUALITY LEARNING FOR A REASONABLE INVESTMENT

That's the mission statement. Sure, there's definition and lots of explanation that can go along with it, but if you know that much you've got a pretty good picture of what's going on, and why.

Look at the first part of the statement: "Quality Learning." What does that mean? Only that every decision of the organization regarding program and resource content and curriculum is dictated by that objective. New seminar? Change in course content? New publication for purchase at the workshop? New workshop leader? One question only: "Will this provide for a quality learning experience?"

Consider: "Reasonable Investment." Companies in this business don't survive long without this aspect in gear. Each decision made is based on the question: "Will this enable us to provide our product for a reasonable investment?"

3

The two parts of this mission statement must function together. National Seminars might offer the greatest educational experience the world has ever seen, but if no one can afford to attend, no one would benefit. Perhaps costs could be reduced so low as to provide a full-day seminar for a very low price, and only a place the size of the New Orleans Superdome could hold the crowds that would attend. But, if the program was poor, no one would benefit and no one would ever come back. No one element can stand alone in the mission statement. It must be complete.

Simple, strong and direct! That's what a mission statement should be.

At **Hewlett Packard's McMinnville, Oregon plant** (a cardiology equipment-manufacturing facility), guests are served coffee in a mug with the company's mission statement printed on the side. It serves as a constant reminder of the division's reason for existence:

"The Cardiology Business Unit (CBU) mission is to become the global, leading supplier of diagnostic cardiology and resuscitation products.

"The CBU will meet its customers' needs and gain market share by being the low-cost supplier of a broad line of profitable products which offer value through quality and best-in-class performance."

Employees of the CBU are enthusiastic about the ways in which the mission statement makes a difference in the quantity and quality of production and the resulting impact on the company's sales figures.

What about a non-profit organization or agency? How can a mission statement work there? Here are two examples.

3

From the **Naval Aviation Depot, Alameda, California**:

"We are a national resource. We provide responsive maintenance, engineering and logistics services in support of our nation's defense.

"Our mission is to support our customers by continually improving our products and services, while providing the highest quality at minimum cost."

This mission statement uses words we associate with the profit-making sector! Customers. Products and services. Highest quality. Minimum cost. Each of these terms is clearly defined so that everyone can understand them. Each employee carries a plastic-laminated mission statement with the defined terms printed on the back.

From **Prince George, British Columbia, Public Schools**:

"We are a Public Community Resource. We provide education for our nation's children. Our mission is to provide quality education and services while supporting individual needs and being responsible to our taxpayers, whose money funds our schools."

Every mission statement quoted represents a clear, specific definition of purpose that guides planning, decision-making and activity; one that's available to every employee in the organization. Communication of this kind creates motivation and commitment on all levels of responsibility.

A mission statement by itself is not a guarantee of organizational success. But, when you realize how a mission statement affects motivation and understanding throughout the workplace, is it any wonder why some organizations move ahead and others stall? Why do some succeed when others fail? Why does a recession force some companies out of business while others grow? As hints of an economic downturn began to appear throughout the country, one executive made this statement.

3

"We actually welcome a recession, because we're strong and well-positioned. If some of our competitors go out of business, it means we'll increase our market share. And all of our people know and understand this."

What is your organization's mission statement? Do you know it? Does it even have one? See what you can find out.

A Departmental or Team Mission Statement

Suppose you go in search of your organization's mission statement and find there's not one ... at least not one that can be easily understood and used by all employees. Even if you are not in a position to redefine that overall statement, you can be instrumental in creating clarity of purpose at the departmental or team level.

Step 1. Meet with your colleagues and co-workers to define the following:

A. Who are your customers (internal and external) by category?

B. What unique expectations does each group have?

C. What could your team do to meet or exceed each of those expectations?

D. How are those efforts to be communicated to your customers?

Step 2. Ask each team member to complete the following statement on a 3 x 5 card. "My vision of a team that works is ..."

Assimilate, merge and modify the responses until group consensus has been reached.

Step 3. Use all the detailed information generated in Steps 1 and 2 to generate your team's mission statement. You'll be amazed at how much more productive and compatible team members will be once your team purpose is clearly defined in operational terms relevant to their daily functions.

What Is YOUR Personal Mission Statement?

Why did you get out of bed this morning? What forces drive you, compel you to action and productivity? Where are you headed in life and why? Who are you, really?

Your personal mission statement should be the guiding instrument of your life. Just as a company needs a mission statement to help make decisions and set direction, so do you. You have the ultimate control over who you are and what you become — to your organization but, more importantly, to yourself.

It's not too late nor one minute too early to do some serious thinking about what your personal mission statement should be. In fact, this is quite possibly the most important thinking you can do in this entire manual to make a difference in how you organize, manage and control your projects and priorities throughout your life.

Wally Amos, the "Famous" chocolate-chip cookie-seller of the same name, put it this way in an interview with Dr. Robert Schuller: "You have to determine exactly what it is you want in life and make it clear and specific. Then you make all your decisions based on the mission statement you develop in answer to that question."

Basically it boils down to this. What do you want to be known for after your death? What would you like your friends, family, co-workers, neighbors, etc., to say about you,

3

your life, your character, and your contributions after your life is over?

Make a list. Contemplate. Then begin by filling in the blanks in the following statement:

_____'s **Personal Mission Statement:**

Can you do that in 25-50 words? Commit it to memory and to heart? Repeat it to anyone who asks? Use this statement as a guide to important decisions about what's important to you, and the best use of your time?

This is where effective planning and decision-making must begin.

Remember to Fine-Tune

Whether it's an organizational or personal mission statement, the statement has been established in a world that is constantly changing.

Every three months, review your mission statement and make the subtle but necessary changes required to keep it current. Perhaps no fine-tuning will be necessary; but if the mission statement is neglected without updating for too long, it will no longer reflect your purpose for existence.

Think back 10 years. Where were you 10 years ago? What has changed in your life since that time? What would your mission statement have been then, compared to what it is now?

If you can imagine the shock that would come from jumping directly from the 10-year-old mission statement to a new one, remember it's possible to avoid that through the quarterly fine-tuning process.

After the Mission Statement — The Next Steps

Once the mission statement is in place, other steps follow as you move up the ladder to results and accomplishment in your life and organization.

- **Long-Term Goals:** What are the 10-, five- and one-year milestones you must reach in order to achieve the purposes of your mission statement? Where do you want to be in 10 years? Five? What must you accomplish in the coming year to make those goals a reality?

- **Short-Term Objectives:** What are the semi-annual, monthly and weekly steps required to reach your goals? Once you know your long-term goals, you must identify shorter-term stepping stones to get you there. What must you do by the end of the next six months? Next month?

- **Strategy:** How are you going to get there? What key areas must you work on?

- **Related Goals: (Optional)** This refers to the side goals that might be helpful in attaining your overall goals. Perhaps taking a course at night would make you better qualified to achieve some of your objectives.

3

- **Measurement:** How will you evaluate what you're doing? What are the boundaries you have to work within? Without a means of measurement, achievement can never be verified, and mileposts are never established to show progress.

- **Action Steps:** Use daily and weekly action lists. What do you need to accomplish today as you move in the direction you want to go? What must you accomplish this week?

- **Implementation:** Stop thinking and do it. As Peter Drucker says, "All planning must eventually degenerate into work for anything to actually happen."

- **Evaluation and Redefinition:** Examine your results and determine what they mean. Are they directing you toward your long-range goals? How do your results fit with your mission statement? Use the FAR method to evaluate and redefine.

FEEDBACK, APPRAISAL AND REVISION

Feedback tells you how you're doing. Develop your own feedback mechanism in addition to the ones your organization may have built in. You need feedback relating to your own goals as well as to how well you're meeting the organization's expectations.

Appraisal is the pivot point — the place where you begin to turn from the past to the future. Lee Iacocca describes such an activity in his autobiography when he talks about a Sunday evening time in his family room at home when he compares the last week's results to his plans for the week, then refocuses his direction ahead to the coming week based on his appraisal.

Focus on measurable results and keep your eye on the target. Look at results every day and appraise your progress weekly and monthly. How closely does your actual performance match your plan? Are you moving toward your end goals at an appropriate pace?

Revision of the plan are action steps for the future to further progress toward the goals. As circumstances and events around you change, your approach to goal achievement may need to shift as well. The more adept you are at identifying these needs and revising your plan, the more successful you will be in reaching your ultimate goals.

When you evaluate and redefine, take a hard look back down at the bottom of the ladder to the mission statement supporting all your plans. Were the results consistent with the mission statement? If so, congratulations, keep it up! If not, what could you do differently to produce results more in line with what your purposes are?

As you can see, the planning process begins and ends with the mission statement. That's why that clarity of purpose is so essential. It fuels your motivation throughout the process!

> *WHEN YOU FAIL TO RELATE*
> *YOUR TODAYS TO YOUR TOMORROWS,*
> *YOU HAVE TO START OVER EVERY DAY!*

3

Understanding Goals and How They Work

The major purpose of this chapter is not to teach you about goal-setting; there are lots of wonderful books devoted exclusively to this process. A significant aspect of priority management, however, is how goal-setting works in relation to the big picture of personal and organizational mission statements.

Goal-setting is work! You may have heard or read someone eloquently telling you how easy it is to set and achieve goals. Don't believe it. Setting goals is a real struggle; but it's a healthy struggle, one that is absolutely essential for success and survival.

The message for us is: Without the struggle of good goal-setting, you will never develop the strength and resolve to achieve the targets you set out ahead of you, and to overcome the setbacks and adversity that inevitably come to a person with a purpose.

Many warm, fulfilling stories come to mind about the importance of the struggle associated with goal-setting. It's exciting, for example, to think about people who are many, many years past what used to be considered "retirement" age who are doing everything but retiring!

When George Burns celebrated his 95th birthday, he had already scheduled a televised extravaganza from the London Palladium to celebrate his 100th birthday! The great conductor Leopold Stokowski died at age 97. He had already made commitments before that time for conducting engagements three years ahead — engagements he would have been 100 years old to make good!

Insurance actuary figures show the life expectancy of a person who has truly retired, with no goals or ambitions remaining, to be less than two years. The two men above are only representative of many people who discover goals to be not only strength-giving, but life-giving! As long as you'll set goals and commit yourself to them, you may eventually wear out, but you'll never rust out.

Three "MUSTs" for Goal Achievement

1. **Commit your goals to paper.** Writing your goals enables you to identify them most clearly, and increases your personal and career commitments. Without writing your goals down, the possibility of achievement drops to nearly zero. Writing your goals:

    *   Makes them concrete. Your goals are not nebulous clouds floating around somewhere in your head, but entities you can see.

    *   Keeps them fresh in your mind. When goals are written, they're seldom forgotten.

    *   Gives you a sense of urgency and commitment. As you look at what you have written, you are constantly encouraged to action.

    *   Makes them measurable. Nothing is more satisfying than looking at a list of goals and actually being able to check them off and reward yourself.

    *   Makes things happen. There's almost a supernatural attraction of written goals to getting results. When Conrad Hilton was a young man, he owned two small hotels (his first hotel was in Cisco, Texas). One day, he read an article about the Waldorf Astoria Hotel in New York, called "the greatest hotel in the world." He clipped a picture of the hotel and placed it under the glass on his desktop saying, "The greatest of them all and one day I'll own it." He looked at that clipping every day. Thirty years later, Conrad

3

Hilton became the first individual (not a corporation) in history to own the Waldorf Astoria Hotel.

Written goals represent the difference between results and good intentions. Harry Truman once remarked the worst thing that could be said of a man was: *"He meant well."*

The more specific your written goals, the more direction they will provide. Where are you going? How will you get there? How will you know when you've arrived?

2. **Strive for progress, not perfection.** Remember the 80-20 rule? When you set your standards unrealistically high or severe, the chance of success disappears.

   You can learn a lesson from Japan here. The Japanese have a principle called *kaizen*, which relates closely to the question. Every day, the objective of each worker is to do his or her job a little bit better than the day before. No quantum leaps! No revolutionary changes! Just a little better than yesterday. And tomorrow, the goal is to do a little better than today.

   Spectacular? No. But amazingly productive. This is how mastery is achieved. And mastery is not perfection. One can be achieved; the other can't and really isn't even necessary. In the year Tom Kite became the first golfer ever to earn one million dollars in one year, he never made a hole-in-one! Did he have a bad year? No, he was a master of his skill, even though he never achieved perfection!

3. **Develop strong interpersonal relationships.** Good interpersonal relationships imply a reciprocity with others. It is seldom possible to achieve goals without the involvement of other people — the "Lone Ranger" approach is rarely successful.

Canada geese give us a clear picture of how we can function together. As a flock of geese flies, several things are happening. First, the formation is always a V shape. The geese at the head of the V have to fly the hardest, breaking through the air while the others in the formation fly in the draft created by the lead goose. Just behind and inside the head of the V you'll frequently notice some geese not in formation. These are the old and the weak. They can fly longer if they never fly on the edge of the formation. The stronger geese do the work.

If you watch long enough, you will also see the lead goose break out of formation and fly to the back of the V, letting another take the point. By sharing the work load, the flock can fly faster and longer as each takes the point position while others rest. If a member of the flock lags behind, another goes back and flies with it. If a goose leaves the formation and goes to the ground, another accompanies it.

Are there people you can call on when help is needed? Are there people who literally block the road to your progress because a relationship is broken or has never formed? Are you willing to rest once in a while and let others fly at the leading edge? Just how connected are you?

3

Three More Questions for Managers: Present and Future

1. **Is this goal worthwhile for the organization?** Is it necessary? Will this goal help you achieve your organizational mission statement? If you can't answer this question with yes, maybe it shouldn't be on your list.

2. **Is it the right time for this goal?** Is it appropriate? This may be a wonderful goal for your organization or department, but is the timing right? Are there other more important objectives at this time? Would energy directed to this goal detract from achieving other goals?

3. **Should you be the one to handle this goal?** Is it efficient? Even though the goal may be right and the timing right, you still need to ask, "Why me?" Is this the best use of your time and energy right now? Is there someone else who could and should be doing this? Is this something you should delegate?

What is the growth trend in your department? The mark of a leader is the growth and development of the people for whom the leader is responsible. What are you delegating? What can you delegate? (More on delegation in Chapters 7 and 10.)

To summarize:

> *GOAL-SETTING DETERMINES WHAT'S IMPORTANT FOR YOU AND ENABLES YOU TO MAKE DECISIONS REGARDING YOUR PRIORITIES.*

3

Marking Your Path

Goal-setting is a struggle to be your own person while a myriad of forces are trying to persuade you to do otherwise. Personal productivity is a by-product of this healthy struggle, for you and your organization.

The Path for Personal Productivity Worksheet can literally function as your map to take you where you want to go. Use it daily as part of your 15-minute-a-day planning session.

Write in your personal mission statement in the space provided at the top and your organizational mission statement in the box at the bottom. Comparing the personal and organizational mission statements can tell you a lot: Are you in the right job? The right organization? The right career? What is your primary work value? How does it compare to the organization's values and objectives? What kind of "match" is or isn't there?

3

Path For Personal Productivity Worksheet*

My Personal Mission Statement:

_____

_____

_____

My Long-Range Goals:

Personal	Work-Related	Leisure-Related
_____	_____	_____
_____	_____	_____
_____	_____	_____

My Goals for the Next Month or Year:

Personal	Work-Related	Leisure-Related
_____	_____	_____
_____	_____	_____
_____	_____	_____

My Goals for the Next Week or Month:

Personal	Work-Related	Leisure-Related
_____	_____	_____
_____	_____	_____
_____	_____	_____

My Top Priorities for Tomorrow:

Personal	Work-Related	Leisure-Related
_____	_____	_____
_____	_____	_____
_____	_____	_____

Note: Your personal mission statement should be re-evaluated quarterly. This process helps you maintain a sense of perspective and balance.

My organization's mission:

*Photocopy before filling in for reuse later.

If the fit isn't really tight, what can you do to change your personal mission statement to align more closely with your organization's? What position should you be seeking within your organization that will enable you to fulfill your personal statement? If the two statements are too far apart, is it time to change organizations?

Note on the Path for Personal Productivity page the statement about reevaluating your personal mission statement every three months. Remember, this is an excellent way to fine-tune your purposes to align them with your needs and your circumstances. Regular reevaluation enables you to stay on top of the circumstances with a currently valid personal mission statement.

The boxes in between the two mission statements are for goals, work-related as well as personal and leisure-related. It's extremely important to have all three to provide balance and fulfillment in all aspects of life. Balance reduces stress which increases motivation which increases the speed with which you make progress toward your goals.

After filling in your personal and organizational mission statement, complete the long-range goals section. Set these as far out as you can realistically visualize. If you can only see 12 months ahead, look only that far. If you can see five years out, great! To keep the chart realistic and attainable, don't go further than five years.

You can't set short-range goals until you know what your long-range goals are. After you've established those long-range targets, think about the next month (if your long-range goals are 12 months out) or year (if they are five years out).

Of course, you can't set goals for the next week or month if you don't know where you're heading in the next month or year, so don't do the third box down until you've finished box 2.

Finally, determine the top priorities for tomorrow. Once again, it's useless to try to determine these without the advantage of seeing the big picture. A common mistake in goal-setting and plotting is to start with today and trying to work in an outward direction. It makes about as much sense as getting into the car and driving, trying to figure out where your destination is, based on what you pass along your way.

Make several photocopies of the blank Personal Productivity Worksheet. Once you're satisfied with the basic information you've put in the first two boxes, make more copies leaving boxes 3 and 4 blank as these will change so frequently. Then include these pages in your work pages as a part of your daily 15 minutes of planning.

Below are several examples of goals in the areas listed on the worksheet included only to stimulate your thinking, not as suggestions. Your own ideas will be much better, much more personal and, much more stimulating to you.

Work-Related

- Get promoted this year
- Become top salesperson in the district
- Pass the CPA examination
- Change careers to better match my mission statement with my job

Personal

- Pay off the mortgage on my house
- Develop one new friendship each month
- Take a class in a subject that interests me
- Learn to control my tendency to procrastinate

Leisure-Related

- Join the garden club
- Get my private pilot's license
- Travel to the South Pacific
- Get selected to appear on a TV show

Your Personal Goals Map

One final way of looking at your goals and mission is the Personal Goals Map. This is a great tool for brainstorming and visualizing your way to success. It's amazing how many people go through life aimlessly wandering around, with no plan or goal, waiting for someone to give them direction.

The Personal Goals Map shows you how you can get a better sense of who you are and where you are in the many different areas of life. It is vitally important to have goals in all the areas listed.

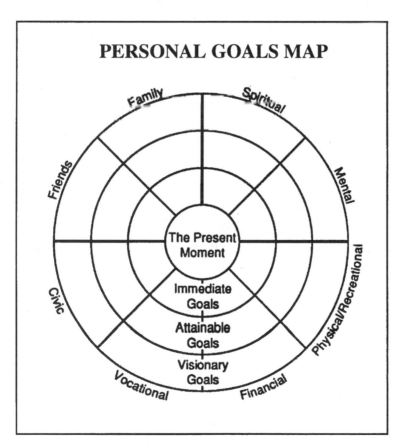

PERSONAL GOALS MAP

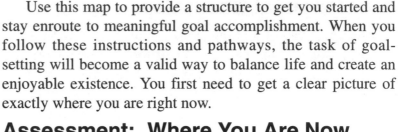

3

Use this map to provide a structure to get you started and stay enroute to meaningful goal accomplishment. When you follow these instructions and pathways, the task of goal-setting will become a valid way to balance life and create an enjoyable existence. You first need to get a clear picture of exactly where you are right now.

Assessment: Where You Are Now

If you can't answer the question, "Where am I now?" it's impossible to determine the direction you want to go.

Directions: You'll need a stack of at least 10 file cards for this self-discovery exercise.

On each card write: "My name is (your name). I am a(n) _____." It should take only a few minutes to complete each of these ten statements differently. Write down your true feelings without analysis, qualification or censorship. Some of them might be negative: overweight. Some of them will merely be factual: stamp collector. Others may reveal positive insights: sensitive, caring person. The only requirement is to be honest. There are no right or wrong answers.

After you've done all the cards, arrange them in order of importance and number them. Add the statement: "This 'I am' is first because _____ ." Do this for all the cards in numerical order.

Finally, to learn something about the person who wrote these cards, ask yourself these questions:

- What do I know about myself from reading these cards?

- What things are most important to me and why?

- Are there things I would enjoy doing with life, but I am not doing now?

- If I had only six months to live, how would I spend my time?

3

The answers to this assessment will tell you a lot about yourself, who you are, what's important to you, and establish where you are right now.

Look outward from the center of the circle in the Personal Goals Map all the way to the edge. Be visionary for a while. What kinds of ultimate goals and accomplishments can you see in the areas on the map? Write them into the appropriate section.

After filling in the outside, once again work your way back in to attainable goals (maybe 12 months out), and determine some immediate goals and steps you can take right now, to move in the direction of the outer edge of the circle. You may have to give up some things to have what you want. Recognize your limitations. You can only do one thing at a time in the present moment. There may be some initial pain or unpleasantness in the present moment as things begin to change. But when you know where you're going and what you want, it's worth it!

Personal knowledge such as this is invaluable in planning and decision-making. Don't put it off!

The Struggle for Goal Compatibility

Goal-setting is a healthy struggle that becomes unhealthy when the goals set are not compatible with each other. Examples:

- The hard-driving business executive loses his or her family in the quest for corporate success.

- The musician chooses career over love.

- The mother is torn between her profession and her children.

- The retired person loses the will to live.

If you pursue certain goals, it may well mean you have to sacrifice something else to attain your objective. *A Passion*

3

for Excellence author Tom Peters observed that if a person truly wants to be at the very top of his or her profession — the Chief Executive Officer, the best-selling author, the award-winning actor or actress, even Volunteer of the Year — it's highly unlikely that goal can be achieved unless that person is willing to throw every bit of energy in that direction, at the expense of other things in life.

Whether you're striving for the top spot or not, always calculate your personal cost as you determine the things you want.

Compatible goals must be written into your plans for success, because achievement if it occurs can be extraordinarily empty without them.

Remember, success comes as a series of small accomplishments rather than as a big break. If you read about an "overnight success" in the business, entertainment or sports world, don't believe it! Most of the opportunities of life are disguised as work, and lots of it.

Copy the planning pages in this chapter right now and begin to make your maps and cut your paths through the woods. You'll be able to organize and manage your priorities with effectiveness you never thought possible.

We were all meant to be achievers. Life is fulfilling and satisfying only as long as you stretch and strive to achieve in some way. When you set a goal, the energy to achieve it comes from within. It's always there, but it's not released until the challenge of a goal is set before you. You are capable of continuing to grow as long as you live. You can continue to learn, to take on new challenges, to discover yourself.

Goal-setting fosters career and mental health. Look at the people around you. Those who are going places in their careers and who have enthusiastic attitudes toward life are the ones with goals. If someone is stagnating in a job or looks at everything with a negative or suspicious attitude, you'll know this is a person without a goal.

Balancing your goals in all areas is quite a juggling act. Additional detail on how to achieve that balance is provided in Chapter 12.

Summary of Key Points

- All planning and goal-setting begins and ends with a mission statement.

- A mission statement must be distinct, stimulating and motivating.

- A personal mission statement and an organizational mission statement should be compatible.

- If your personal and organizational mission statements are not compatible, think about your options.

- If you don't know your organization's mission statement, ask!

- If your organization does not have a mission statement, write one.

- Establish a departmental or team mission statement.

- Know and follow the steps of planning to attain your goals and objectives.

- Revision of your plan is vital to ultimate success in any endeavor.

- Goal-setting is work, but the struggle is essential to strength and resolve.

- Putting a goal in writing helps you achieve it.

- People need each other! Work on developing "connectedness" with others to obtain their help and support.

3

Putting Mission Statements and Goals to Work in Your Life

1. What is your organization's mission statement? Get a copy and post it in your office.

2. How does your job relate to that mission statement? What can you do every day to support that vision?

3. Does your personal mission statement fit with the one for your organization? If not, what will you do?

4. List some people you know who are still thriving late in life. Who are they? What are their goals? What has kept them motivated? Interview them and see what you can learn and emulate.

5. Do you have long-term and short-term goals for your career and your personal life? Are they committed to paper? If not, start on them now. If so, when were they last reviewed and updated? Do it now.

6. Where are you now? Based on your 10 or more index cards from the assessment, what things are most important to you?

7. Have you used that information to complete your Personal Goals Map? If so, in which areas will you work? If not, when will you complete it?

8. Chart a 30-day course of action. Reassess your progress in 30 days and modify your plan.

Action TNT — Today Not Tomorrow

No one ever built a reputation based on what they were going to do tomorrow.

3

MY SLIGHT-EDGE IDEAS
ABOUT LONG-RANGE PLANNING:

CHAPTER 4

Planning for Success

"He who every morning plans the transactions of the day, and follows out that plan, carries a thread that will guide him through the labyrinth of the most busy life."

Victor Hugo

People don't accidentally succeed at juggling the demands of life. Success has little to do with luck. It has to do with planning. *If you think you don't have time to plan, consider this: Planning actually gives you more time.*

You have, no doubt, experienced situations like this: "If only I had thought to bring this tool, the job would be a cinch!" "Why didn't I remember to check with Customer B while I was on that side of town. Now I will have to make two trips!" Time is wasted every day for lack of a plan!

Planning gives you leverage. The financial world uses the word leverage as a way of measuring how much can be controlled with personal investment. For example, if you bought a $150,000 house and paid $30,000 down, you are considered to be leveraging $150,000 in assets with your investment. Each dollar you put in is actually controlling five dollars. If you could buy that same house for just a $15,000 down payment, each of your dollars would then control 10. The more of someone else's money you can use and still have control of the asset, the greater your leverage.

4

It makes sense in finance, and it certainly makes sense in planning. Time spent in planning literally allows you to control more of the remainder of your time. In fact, it actually gives time back.

Time-effectiveness studies conducted by DuPont support this concept: For every one minute spent in planning, the time required to complete an activity is reduced by three to four minutes. Spend 10 minutes, reduce completion time by 30 to 40 minutes. Spend an hour, reduce by three to four hours! That's leverage!

When properly used, 15 minutes of planning can effectively control your time for an entire day. One quarter hour controls eight hours!

Assessment: Current Planning Habits

Directions: To learn something about your present orientation to planning, take a moment to go over this quiz, circling the answer that best describes your orientation.

	Agree	Unsure	Disagree
I take regular time for planning every working day	3	2	1
I have a personally chosen calendar or organizational system	3	2	1
Before tackling a project, I carefully plan what it should accomplish	3	2	1
I usually complete a *Daily Action List*	3	2	1
I do not have difficulty making decisions	3	2	1
I daily spend time on projects with long-term benefits	3	2	1
The gas tank in my car is presently at least half full	3	2	1
I know exactly when my most productive time of the day is	3	2	1
I know my most important project for tomorrow	3	2	1
I have a current Master Project List	3	2	1

4

Interpretation:

25 or more: You have a plan, and are working your plan

15 to 24:   Sometimes your day gets the better of you

less than 15:   How are you holding up under your present crisis?

The Benefits of Planning

Planning is truly the key to managing our priorities better. There are many advantages to planning, including the following:

- **Planning makes things happen.** With no plan, chaos reigns. Events are left to chance. There's no priority and no way to measure accomplishment. Effective planning ensures completion of your priorities; it increases your chance of achieving success and recognition, no matter what the project. Does that frighten you? Does it seem risky? With an intelligent plan, it shouldn't. In fact, you will never have control over your own life until you understand and attain the results possible through planning!

Thoreau said:

> *"IT'S NOT ENOUGH TO BE BUSY.*
> *THE QUESTION IS: WHAT ARE WE*
> *BUSY ABOUT?"*

4

- **Planning promotes job and career advancement.**
  A simple illustration will suffice here: You are considering two people for promotion. One is a wonderful human being, but never quite has a clear purpose or direction. Effort is being expended, but there seems to be no real sense of what is important.

  The other is continually planning the work and working the plan. Things really happen around this person. Who would you choose?

- **Planning provides the necessary framework for decision-making.** Did you ever wonder why some people approach a decision with confidence and assurance when so many others start to panic and perspire?

  Once again, the key is a plan. With a plan, you can see how events and activities fit in. With a well-thought plan, good decisions can be made even when crises arise and you must make quick decisions with limited information.

- **Planning will reduce crises.** The word here is *reduce*, not eliminate. That's because there are two kinds of crises: legitimate ones and false ones. Certain events can't be foreseen, so trying to plan around them is impossible.

  At work, you can't anticipate a personal emergency that calls your key employee away from the job in the middle of the day. But through effective planning, you can anticipate the absence of an employee who has an occasional emergency. Good planning prevents you from counting on 100% availability.

  Many crises occur simply because somebody failed to plan; most of these are completely avoidable. Some crises occur that can't be avoided; and you must have a contingency plan to handle them.

4

- **Planning gives direction to energy.** A rodeo bronco horse has lots of energy, but no direction. Someone attempting to ride this creature has to literally hang on for dear life. Once the horse has been trained and becomes familiar with structure and discipline, its energy can be channeled into positive production, i.e., work or to be ridden. So it is with a plan. You control the energy rather than allowing the energy to simply "go with the flow."

Obstacles to Planning

Six common obstacles prevent many people from planning. Understanding the truth behind planning obstacles can help you avoid the consequences of poor or inadequate planning.

OBSTACLE #1: Day-to-day operations. Sometimes it's hard to see beyond the current avalanche of paper or beyond the next crisis. But time taken to plan is *invested* to maximize your efficiency in handling the ongoing critical issues. Once again, sometimes the feeling can be: "I'm simply too busy to stop to plan." Remember the leverage factor when such thoughts creep into your mind!

Firefighters go to sleep at the fire station, but not before they have laid out their clothes on the floor next to the bed. The day-to-day operation of dressing is already considered, and these professionals have reduced the activity to a quick, predetermined process.

Could you move more efficiently in the morning if you developed the same habit? How much time do you spend after getting up making clothing decisions? How much time do you spend trying to find the clothes you want? What if the power went off during the night and you unintentionally overslept? Would adopting the firefighters' plan help minimize the negative effects?

It's not necessary to deal with the nuts and bolts of your day-to-day operations here. But consider why you are doing the things you do. In the firehouse illustration, you're not interested in how the clothes are laid out, or what those clothes are. The question is: Why do firefighters do that? Obviously, they invest the time up front to facilitate their response when they are called to action.

Examine your own activities. Are they all necessary? Do they have to be done daily? Is this merely a habit developed for a reason that is no longer valid? Can any activity be eliminated, or delegated without negative effects?

Do you get important correspondence finished to take to the mail room at 11:00 every morning? Are you doing this because that's what the person who held the job before you always did?

Perhaps at one time the mail carrier arrived at the office at that time every day. But now the company has a post office box where mail is picked up at 6:00 a.m. and outgoing mail is dropped off at 6:00 p.m. So why are you organizing your day around getting correspondence to the mail room by 11:00? It's easy to keep doing something just because "it's the way it has always been done"! But why do you do it?

OBSTACLE #2: Lack of immediate satisfaction. We live in a society where everyone wants everything now, if not sooner. Why save money to buy something when a plastic card allows you to have it now?

Sociologist Robert Merton noted *successful people* often exhibit a behavior he termed as the Deferred Gratification Pattern. This behavior reflects *a willingness to put off something now and invest more work, energy or money to attain something better in the future*. Rather than being disenchanted, logically examine the situation; the hidden price tag is usually the real benefit of waiting.

4

Keep this in mind as you look at the early results of the plans you make. Don't be deceived or discouraged if your efforts don't result in immediate payoff. Even if it's a good plan, it may take a while. If you follow the Ten Tips for a Fast Start while you are developing your plan, you can have immediate gratification and long-term success.

OBSTACLE #3: What, more paperwork? Not really. More thinking creates less paper. Though it may seem to the contrary, planning actually works to your advantage. With planning, you can make decisions more quickly and effectively, actually reducing the amount of paper you have to handle on the job.

OBSTACLE #4: Habits. Habits are acquired and can be reinforced or changed. If failure to adopt the planning habit is your problem, you're only 30 days away from never worrying about it again. Make the choice today, commit to it, and make planning one of your acquired daily habits.

OBSTACLE #5: The fear of failure. You may be thinking, "What will happen if I really make the effort here? What if I sincerely try to change my patterns and spend more time each day planning my activities, and I have nothing to show for it? I'll feel even worse than I do now, because I've tried it and failed."

This simply can't happen! Guaranteed. How much more successful you will be depends on where you are now and how much effort goes into your planning program. But you will be more effective and regain considerably more control over your day. Set realistic expectations for improvement with small steps rather than quantum leaps. Small things over time make the difference.

Some people are not so much afraid of failing as they are of succeeding. *Fear of success* can also deter actively implementing plans. Relax. You'll grow in so many ways as planning becomes a part of your life that you'll be prepared for the greater responsibility that accompanies success. Plus, you'll know how to plan to accommodate the new challenges!

OBSTACLE #6: Planning is work! True, but work can be fun. If you believe there is only unpleasantness in work, you will shortchange yourself of life's satisfaction. Besides, the most pleasant part of planning is thinking about the benefits you're going to receive as a result of what you're doing!

Important or Urgent?

Have you ever been in a situation where a trivial matter suddenly became a major problem that seemed to dominate every aspect of your life? Have you ever spent a day "putting out fires" and gone home wondering what you accomplished? Experiences like these are convincing testimonials to the absolute necessity of planning. These are the times when we become subjects to the *tyranny of the urgent*.

There's a world of difference between important and urgent. Important, as defined in the dictionary, is something significant and consequential. Under "urgent" we find the words insistent and pressing. Nowhere are words like significant and consequential to be found in the definition of urgent! The things we must pay attention to should be items that are significant and that have consequence. If your energy is directed primarily to activities that are insistent or pressing, your energy is misdirected!

4

1 **URGENT AND IMPORTANT**	2 **IMPORTANT BUT NOT URGENT**
3 **URGENT BUT NOT IMPORTANT**	4 **NOT URGENT AND NOT IMPORTANT**

Quadrant 1: Urgent and Important. These are the crises of life. When you spend the day "putting out fires," you spend the day in Quadrant 1. You're handling all those things that are significant and consequential as well as insistent and pressing. These are items that need to be done and they have to be done now. Time spent here is REACTIVE. More than 80 percent of the people you know spend most of their time here. All their effort and work accounts for less than 20 percent of all that is accomplished.

Quadrant 2: Important but Not Urgent. These are the items that are all too easily put off until tomorrow. Things that have long-term consequence but are not currently pressing. Tasks related to preservation, prevention, growth and opportunity development would all fit here. These are items that really need to be done but are put off until an unspecified "tomorrow." Frequently, tomorrow never comes. These important but not urgent tasks are ignored until they jump out of Quadrant 2 into Quadrant 1 and they become the crisis of the moment.

A small investment of time early on in Quadrant 2 could avoid a large investment of time when the issue reaches Quadrant 1. "An ounce of prevention is worth a pound of cure." This is taking a PROACTIVE role in making things happen. These are included in the 20 percent of activities that will produce 80 percent of your results.

Quadrant 3: Urgent but Not Important. These are the items that are clamoring for your attention but they are not important in your priority assessment. Frequently, these are other people's problems. Do you ever find yourself handling things that other people should be doing? Do you find it difficult to decline when someone asks you to do something they should be handling themselves? If so, you are wasting time in Quadrant 3 that would be better spent in Quadrant 2.

Quadrant 4: Not Urgent and Not Important. Trivial, daily items and wasted time that may need to be done, but that do not move you toward your goals would fall here. Have you ever gone into work an hour early to get a jump on the day? You get a cup of coffee and head for your office. On the way, you stop to speak to a colleague who is also in early and pass the time about your activities the previous evening. When you finally get back to your office and settle in at your desk, you discover your coffee cup is empty. Off you go to get another cup and the cycle begins again. What has happened to that extra hour? Instead of being devoted to Quadrant 2 activities, you have fallen directly into Quadrant 4.

Effective planning can help you minimize the time you spend in Quadrants 1, 3, and 4 and maximize the time you have for doing what is really important. Making that major shift can be done in four steps.

4

Step 1: Identify wasted moments throughout your day and use them more effectively. This will give you more chunks of usable time for Quadrant 2 projects. (Details in Chapters 7 and 8.)

Step 2: Learn to say no to other people's requests for your time. (See Chapter 6.)

Step 3: Identify what is truly important. What are the priority items and can you rank them in priority order? (Refer to Chapter 5 for assistance.)

Step 4: Commit to a PLAN that efficiently uses your prime time.

Let's suppose tomorrow is a super day for you, and you accomplish all the items on your list before the end of the day. What should you do next? Lest you get so caught up in accomplishment that everything else is forgotten, remember the basic human need for reward. When you've finished your list, take a little time to relish the feeling of accomplishment so vital to mental health and well-being. Reward yourself with a cup of coffee or a few minutes of exercising or by reading an article that interests you. Then consider what might be next on your list and start again!

Maximize Productivity in Your Prime Time

No one operates all day at the same level of energy. Each person has his or her own ups and downs, and for each person those occur at different times of the day. People frequently make statements that indicate they have a basic idea about themselves and those around them. You may hear someone say, "I'm a morning person. I like to get up and get moving around quickly." About others you might say, "She's really a night owl. It seems the later it is, the more energy she has."

4

There's truth in both of those statements. In order to effectively use the time available, you first need to take a look at yourself and your habits. Do you know what and when your prime time is? Find out using the next worksheet. Even if you already have a feel for the answers, complete the worksheet over several days to verify the accuracy of your assessment.

4

WORKSHEET—Your Personal Prime Time

Directions: Divide your day into two-hour segments, and you will learn a lot about when you function better. In the graph below, plot an X in the appropriate box for each two-hour segment to indicate whether you have a high, medium or low level of energy during a typical day at work.

TIME OF DAY							
Energy Level	6-8 am	8-10 am	10 am-12 pm	12 pm-2 pm	2-4 pm	4-6 pm	6-8 pm
HIGH							
MEDIUM							
LOW							

4

Once the chart is filled in with the Xs in the appropriate boxes, you can graph a typical day by connecting the marks to see how each day has its own natural ups and downs. Some of the time segments probably don't correspond to the eight hours that constitute the core of your working day. By drawing vertical lines at the beginning and ending hours of your work schedule, you can see how much of that energy flows into the hours you are on your company's payroll.

Now, of the times you indicated as high energy, pick the two-hour segment of the day when you believe your greatest amount of energy and concentration is available. This is called your prime time, the time when you are at your physical or mental peak. Formal studies have shown the time at which internal (physical) and external (mental) energy is most likely to come together for many people is about 10:30 a.m. Informal surveys indicate that about 80 percent of all people experience prime time during the morning hours.

The ideal is to do activities that are the most important and require the greatest amount of energy and concentration during your personal prime time.

Once you know when your prime time occurs, there are three things you must do:

1. **RESPECT your prime time.** Don't do the trivial. Don't allow yourself to file, straighten your desk or take a coffee break during your prime time because you're putting off starting that difficult project. Discipline yourself to stay on track.

2. **PROTECT your prime time.** Actually block it off on your daily calendar so the unimportant activities don't crowd into these two hours. Forward your phone to voice mail and close your door or otherwise signal that you are unavailable. Don't allow others to waste these most valuable, productive hours.

4

3. **DIRECT your prime time.** Schedule the most important things of your day, the ones that require the most energy and concentration, into prime time.

Can you change your prime time, once you know what it is? Yes! Sometimes your best times are not convenient for others around you. Perhaps your best time occurs outside normal working hours. It's possible to change because the habits you have developed over your lifetime have shaped much of who you are. Habits can be formed, and habits can be changed.

Is your greatest energy period occurring after work hours? Do you have all kinds of trouble getting started in the morning? Often a change in when you go to bed at night and when you get up can make a big difference here. You might not want to try to change everything all at once. Try moving both times ahead 30 minutes at a time and adjusting for the move. After you've done that four times, you will have altered your sleeping pattern by two hours.

Increased productivity may be as easy as consciously concentrating key activities into certain times of the day, whether you think you have the energy for them or not. Doing this often enough can alter your patterns of energy as new habits begin to evolve.

Whatever your pattern of energy, one habit applied to your daily routine will make an incredible difference in your productivity, accomplishments and energy during the entire day.

TACKLE THE WORST FIRST.

4

Hard to do? Maybe for a while, but after you've developed a strong new habit of doing this, you'll be thrilled with what it can do for your entire day.

Imagine what a difference it will make to have the most difficult task out of the way at the beginning of your day! While the others at work are trying to figure out where they are and what they're going to do first, you'll have taken on that tough project and be well on your way to completing it. The surge of energy you'll have with that wonderful sense of accomplishment after you've finished will make everything else easy. Your day will be a pleasant coast with the major project already out of the way.

Remember a day when you had a tough project that had to be done that day, but you kept putting it off? What a negative energy drain it turned out to be. Anticipation turned to anxiety, then to fear, finally to dread. By the time you decided to get going, you were exhausted. And then, it seemed easier just to reschedule the task for tomorrow. All that energy was expended for nothing.

Of course, the first two hours of your day may not be your prime time. Once you develop the habit of doing your most difficult task first, you'll find that early morning energy level rises. Plus, you may still find your later prime time is still there, making you ready for another surge of productivity toward the end of the day.

The 15 Most Important Minutes of Any Day

It takes only 15 minutes to leverage an entire working day. Block off 15 minutes on your calendar every day. Guard it with your life. No activity on your list requires more protection than this one. Use it, along with other planning tools you have to make each day one of purpose, meaning, direction and accomplishment.

4

While many people choose the first 15 minutes of the day for this daily planning period, we recommend putting it at the end of the previous day instead. Planning at the end of the day has three major advantages:

1. **You make your momentum work for you, rather than suffering the effects of inertia.** The ideas will be much fresher, since you have been at work all day and are well aware of what you have and have not already accomplished.

2. **Doing this at the end of the day will give you a sense of closure on the day.** When you've finished your 15-minute planning session, you will be able to leave work with a true sense of completion, having accomplished the last item on your list. Plus, you'll be able to enjoy your free time and sleep well without worrying about things you need to remember to do at work the next day.

3. **Planning at the end of the day will enable you not only to identify the most important task of the upcoming day, but will allow you to jump in right away the next morning and take on that task immediately.** While others are still trying to find the tops of their desks or drawing that first cup of coffee in the lounge, you can already be on your way to a productive day.

Even if additional items come up overnight, you will spend less time inputting the newly acquired information the next day by not having to start at ground zero.

Dramatic productivity improvements will come from these 15 minutes a day. Use them wisely everyday.

4

The Tools

Each of us has a number tools we can use to make planning work for us. While we may use them in somewhat different ways depending on the nature of our work, they benefit all of us. The fundamental point of this section is this:

> *IF YOU WANT SOMETHING TO HAPPEN,*
> *YOU HAVE TO MAKE A PLACE*
> *FOR IT TO HAPPEN!*

The Appointment Calendar

You make commitments to others each day, and you probably log those commitments on your appointment calendar.

Do you have a meeting scheduled? Meeting a business associate for lunch? Appointments to call on clients? A phone call to someone available only at a certain time? An airplane departure time? Put it in the calendar. Whether you choose a paper calendar or an electronic one is your choice.

There are many tools available. Some of the most comprehensive paper calendar/planning systems are available from Franklin Quest®, Day Runner®, Day-Timers®, and Time/Design®. Evaluate your options and obtain the simplest one that meets your specific needs.

4

The Lists: Two Systems

System #1: The Traditional System — Daily Action and Master Lists

On the daily action list, note all the specific projects and activities that you need to accomplish on that particular day ranked and prioritized (Chapter 5 will explain this further) and listed in such a way that they can be checked off or crossed out after completion.

In looking at this list, if there are items that should be done by someone else, assign those items and get them off your list. Anything with a specific time or deadline can be put on the calendar, including your prime time activity and first activity of the day. What will remain after that time is what you have chosen to do that day, based on available time and priorities.

1. Mark each activity: high, medium or low, based on the amount of energy required, and schedule it according to your energy flow of the day. Don't open the routine mail during your prime time, and don't write the most important letter of the month at a low-energy period.

2. Actually assign a time of day to each item according to when you want to work on it, once again basing your decisions on energy level. If you use the time column this way, you could also then transfer these items to your calendar.

3. Use the time column to conservatively estimate how long each activity requires, which will enable you to create a realistic, achievable list.

As simple as the daily action list is, there are two common mistakes made regularly that keep the list from being fully effective.

1. **Unrealistic Time Projections.**

   Make sure your list contains only as many activities as time will allow. This can be done simply by estimating the amount of time each task requires and writing the time on the list. It's much better to add to your list again later in the day if you've completed everything on it than to remain frustrated by an unrealistic and uncompleted list.

2. **The Calendar Factor Oversight.**

   Even though you may be at work for eight hours on a given day, those eight hours usually do not represent totally discretionary time. What's already on your calendar? If you have three hours committed on your calendar in meetings and appointments, you no longer have eight hours available to you. Once again, factor in the time already committed to other people and be realistic about it.

The master list works as a "project warehouse" where you can store just that kind of item — the things you want to do eventually, even though you know you won't do them today.

Divide your master list into two categories: business and personal. Any time you get an idea of something you want to do, or recognize something that needs to be done, immediately write it on your list in the appropriate category. Then, as you plan the upcoming day, first look at your calendar to determine how much discretionary time you have. Next, look at your Daily Action List for the past day. Anything you didn't complete either goes on today's list or send it back to the "warehouse" if you don't want to work on it again.

Then look at your master list and add to the Daily Action List things you want to accomplish on this day, making realistic time estimates. Once you've moved something from the master list to the Daily Action List, cross it off the master list. In this way, you have to remember something in only one place.

To keep your master list to a workable size, use a three-ring binder. Divide the list into work-related and personal-related categories. If nearly all the items on a page have been crossed out, remove that page and place it in the inactive section after rewriting the items yet to be done on a current page.

Saving the completed pages can provide great motivation and feedback. The completed pages represent a list of accomplishments and keeps a résumé up-to-date. This also provides valuable information about how much you're doing when additional responsibilities are taken on without others being given up. Upon entering a new job, the list can provide valuable reminders of the steps that go into the completion of the task.

System #2: The Brain Clear Way

Remember the mind dump recommended in the Ten Tips for a Fast Start? If you did it, you already know how well this system works. If you haven't started yet, you're in for a treat.

This system breaks down the daily action list and the master list in different ways. Many people find this revised method gives them more specific direction, thereby decreasing wasted transition time between tasks.

Make four lists in addition to using your calendar:

- **Projects List** — all ongoing
- **Next Actions List** — itemizes next step(s) to be taken on all active projects
- **Waiting List** — records all items that must come from someone else
- **Someday/Maybe List** — all discretionary tasks

The projects list itemizes all the projects you are currently juggling. At a glance you get the big picture.

The next actions list is key to your ongoing productivity. No longer do you have to mentally go back to where you left off on a task and figure out what to do next. You've already noted it in the next actions list. Whenever you quit working on something, jot down on the next actions list what needs to happen next. Then when that item is once again the priority, you can get to work with no lost time.

The waiting list lets you quit fretting about keeping up with all the things other people have promised to you or that you need to be able to move forward on a project. When you make a request of someone, note it on your waiting list. When you must wait for some specific event to pass before moving on, note that event. This way you have all your mental energy available to focus on the active tasks at hand.

The someday/maybe list is the parking lot of the projects to be considered for the future, hare-brained schemes that cross your mind and all other discretionary items.

Keeping these lists up-to-date is easy and effective in improving your productivity whether you choose a paper-based or computer-based format.

4

Planning is very rarely a solo performance. Few of us are blessed with the opportunity to make our list each day without considering the needs and priorities of others. These planning tools make excellent visuals in presenting your priorities and decisions to others.

Paper or Electronic?

The computer has enormous potential for increasing your organizational productivity. The more you understand it, work with it, and explore the power it provides, the better able you'll be to maximize your personal organization system.

Creating a personal organization system using your computer to complement your paper-based system will be an ongoing process. Computer organizing software is also abundant. Check the programs already in your computer. What kinds of organizing systems are already available to you? Where can you obtain detailed information on their most efficient use?

If you are in the market to purchase planning software, you must consider exactly what you want it to be able to do for you. Do you want it to maintain your schedule only or become the central focus of your organizational scheme? If the former, any scheduling or planning package can do that sufficiently. If the latter, many more evaluations must be made. Does the program being evaluated:

- Communicate with others via e-mail, telephone, fax, group scheduling and real-time conferencing?
- Provide Internet connectivity, Internet mail, news and shared calendaring?
- Organize all types of communications into one application?

4

- Interact with your current mail and communications packages, or will upgrades or conversions be required?

- Provide access to an overview of the day, a summary of upcoming meetings, deadlines and number of overnight e-mails received on one screen without requiring switching back and forth?

- Enhance e-mail management and prioritization by identifying and dealing with junk mail? Automatically highlight, file, forward and flag incoming and outgoing mail?

- Have a follow-up flag system for tracking item completion?

- Include a meeting planner that easily schedules group meetings (face to face or real time Internet conferences), selects attendees, checks available times, and sends meeting announcements?

- Provide a contact manager that can dial the phone, send e-mail or a fax, or leap to a Web site?

- Have a word processor for letters and reports?

- Have the ability to pull information from various places and create a report for you?

The list could go on ad infinitum. These types of software packages are multiplying fast. Check the Internet for the latest state of the art edition. Symantec, Microsoft, and Lotus are good places to start.

Obviously, the computer can manage many things simultaneously and very effectively. The key is your comfort level and commitment to using the technology. Virtually all the planning and prioritization tools presented throughout this book can be placed in or used by the computer. The key is to develop for yourself a seamless system for integrating your paper tools with your electronic ones. For instance:

4

- Be sure you can see all your next actions in one place (usually on paper). If some are on paper and some in the computer, some will fall between the cracks.

- Record and track reminders about computer files that still need your attention. With the computer's awesome ability to store endless items, documents in process can fall into a black hole if they are not carefully tracked and monitored.

- Use a word processing program to create, store and back up lists. Both Windows and Mac-based processors can easily design custom paper forms for your paper organizing systems. Set up a table the size of your organizer paper, use the Format command to print lines on it, type in titles and headings and print copies as you need them.

- Be sure to purge your entire computer file system regularly. Scan your directories periodically and trash or archive onto disk everything not currently in use.

Many find a paper tracking system is an excellent way to track all the work that you have done ... on your computer. Develop your own combination to match your individual work style.

Adjunct Computer Devices

With the explosion of computer technology has come an explosion of the number and types of personal computer assistant devices available, from credit card size to pocket size to the larger hand-held. Selecting the right one is essential if you are to make it work productively for you.

First you must know exactly what you want it to do and how you will use it. If you're only looking for a pocket organizer that provides easy access to your calendar and contact information, you might choose one of the palm-sized devices. If you need to do more extensive computing such as word processing or Internet browsing, consider a larger, more expensive keyboard-based model. They offer greater input and output capabilities, larger displays, and generally a number of other bells and whistles.

Many excellent products are available from reputable manufacturers (3Com, Casio, Franklin, NEC, Toshiba, Hewlett Packard, to name a few). Here are some things to consider when making your hand-held device decisions.

- Size? Weight?

- Keyboard? Layout? Number pad?

- Screen size? Monochrome or color? Resolution?

- Battery life? (expect less) AC adapter included?

- Onc-handed operation possible?

- Quick launch buttons?

- Voice enabled?

- Handwriting recognition software?

- VGA output port?

- How much RAM? Expandability?

- Integrated slot for memory cards? Modem? Pager card?

- Printer drivers? What printers?

- Specific upload and download capabilities and limitations?

- Is synchronization automatic?

- What is the built-in software?

- Linking capabilities — serial cables, infrared, other wireless?

- What desktop PIMs and contact managers is it designed to sync with?

4

4

- Do word processing files keep their formatting when moved between handheld and desktop PCs?

- Ability to survive being dropped? Check port covers, attachments, hinges and the docking mechanism for sturdiness, fit and finish.

Never before have there been so many time-saving devices and so many people with so little time. Investing the dollars in electronic organizing aids is well worth the expenditure if you'll commit to taking the time necessary to really learn how to use them to maximize your productivity. If you're having difficulty getting the most out of your PC and are simply not that comfortable with technological innovations, perhaps now is not the time to invest in another electronic tool. Master what you have access to already; then move up to the next level.

Making It Work

CONCERN	REASON	STRATEGY
not enough time to plan	don't understand "leverage"	learn: one minute of planning saves 3-4 minutes' work
Daily Action List unfinished	too many activities	prioritize tasks
Daily Action List unfinished	unrealistic time estimates	estimate conservatively, allow for interruptions
Daily Action List unfinished	not enough time	count only discretionary, unscheduled hours available
Daily Action List unfinished	contains long-term projects	start to "warehouse" projects
insistent, pressing and imperative demands	small matter left undone has become urgent	pay attention: don't neglect minor details of life
feeling tired, unfulfilled	no mental breaks	reward yourself for finishing projects and lists
difficult to concentrate on tough jobs	low-energy time of day	know your prime time, work toughest tasks then
worry about job and tasks when away from work	no plan; activities not written out	plan at end of day for following work day

4

4

Summary of Key Points

- Planning allows you to leverage your time at three to four minutes saved for each minute spent planning.

- The more time you plan, the more unencumbered time you will have.

- Planning is essential for job and career advancement.

- Decision-making is easier when you have planned first.

- Energy can be directed productively with a well-made plan.

- Analyze your day-to-day operations to identify tasks better left undone.

- Focus on the important.

- Urgent things are not always important.

- Pay attention to minor matters to keep them from becoming urgent.

- When a task is urgent, it takes complete control of your life.

- Know your prime time and direct the day's most challenging projects into that time frame.

- Like any developed habit, energy levels during the day can be changed through regular corrective action.

- Do your toughest job first, and the rest of the day will be a piece of cake!

- Plan tomorrow at the end of today, and enjoy relaxation and freedom tonight.

- Consider the daily action and master lists and the projects, next actions, waiting and someday/maybe lists.

- Excellent personal organization systems are available, both paper and computer.

- Electronic personal assistant devices are also available for the technologically sophisticated.

4

Putting Planning to Work in Your Life

4

1. WORKSHEET — Planning for the Important

Think about your next working day for a moment and then list below six things you want to get done tomorrow:

a. _____

b. _____

c. _____

d. _____

e. _____

f. _____

Analyze your list:

- Are some of these items day-to-day operations? Which would be on your list virtually every day?

- Are some of these items relatively unimportant now but could become urgent if neglected too long?

- Are some on the urgent list now because of previous neglect?

- Are you putting out fires or taking steps to prevent them?

- Do any of these activities fall into the long-range category? What steps, if taken now, can make life easier and more productive down the road?

2. Make five copies of the Prime Time Worksheet you previously completed. Track your energy levels for one week.

3. What did you discover is your prime time? Identify three things you will do to respect it. Exactly what steps will you take to protect it?

4. Set aside the last 15 minutes of every day for the next two weeks for planning. Keep it up even if your first attempts at organizing your upcoming day are less than spectacularly successful. Remember, "Anything worth doing well is worth doing badly until you can learn to do it right."

5. Chart a 30-day course of action. Reassess your progress in 30 days and modify your plan.

Action TNT — Today Not Tomorrow

No one ever built a reputation based on what they were going to do tomorrow.

4

4

MY SLIGHT-EDGE IDEAS
ABOUT PLANNING FOR SUCCESS:

C HAPTER 5

Setting Priorities

"The main thing is to keep the main thing the main thing."

Patricia Wilson, Living in Excellence

"I'll try to get that done."

"If I have a chance, I'll put it on my list of things to do."

Sound familiar? Quit trying and either commit to do it or forget it. Get out of limbo. It's sapping your effectiveness and your ability to focus on the real priority issues at hand.

As far back as the early 1900s, Victor Pareto explained why a priority system was so important in securing effectiveness. As you recall, his rule, when applied to setting priorities, states that 80 percent of the value of a group of items is generally concentrated in only 20 percent of the items. In other words:

> ***YOU CAN BE 80 PERCENT EFFECTIVE BY ACHIEVING 20 PERCENT OF YOUR GOALS!!***

If you have a Daily Action List of 10 items, you can expect to be 80 percent effective by successfully completing only the two most important items on the list. To be effective you must concentrate on the most important items. You must make a commitment to your commitment to focus on true priority items.

Ivy Lee was a management consultant who helped Bethlehem Steel in 1904. Mr. Lee made an unscheduled visit to Bethlehem's president, Charles Schwab, and said, "Mr. Schwab, I have an idea that I believe will increase productivity at Bethlehem Steel, and I'm going to share it with you. Since I've just dropped in on you today, I don't expect you to pay me. So, here are my conditions: Use the idea yourself first. If it has any value for you, then share it with your people. If you feel the idea was worthwhile, and you want to pay me for it, then pay me what you think it was worth."

"Sounds like I can't lose," said Schwab. "What's the idea?"

"Simple. At the beginning of every day, list in ranked order the six most important things you have to do. Then go to work on number one, and continue to work until you're finished.

"When you've finished the first task, reevaluate the other five items to make sure nothing has changed the ranking. Then go to work on number two. When it's done, re-evaluate, then work on number three.

"If the day ends and you haven't finished all six, don't worry. You wouldn't have gotten all six done using any other method, either. And, you did, in fact, do the most important things on your list.

"Even if the day goes by and you don't even finish number one, remember, you were still working on the most important thing you had to do."

Schwab thanked him and Lee left the office. Several months later, Lee received a check from Charles Schwab for

5

"Keep your commitment to your commitment."

—Dr. Robert L. Lorber

$25,000 along with this note: "Thank you very much. This has been the most important idea I've received all year."

Later, as the story of this meeting began to make its rounds in business circles, people would often come up to Schwab and say, "Why did you pay so much money for such a simple idea?"

Schwab's answer was always the same: "I paid as much as I did because that simple idea has made the difference between where my company was then and where it is now — the most profitable private corporation in the United States!"

Choose what's most important to you and do it first. It's that simple. The hard part is deciding what is most important.

5

Assessment: Do You Keep Your Commitment to Your Commitment?

5

Choose one response to each question:

ALWAYS, USUALLY, SOMETIMES, INFREQUENTLY, NEVER

1. Do you set goals? _____

   Comments:

2. Have you analyzed your present commitments? _____

   Comments:

3. Have you inventoried how you plan spending your time, and how you actually DO spend it daily? _____

   Comments:

4. Do you ask yourself, "What's the best use of my time, energy and skills?"
   _____

   Comments:

5. Do you know your calendar of appointments? _____

   Comments:

6. Are your goals and objectives in writing? (Or do they turn out to be wishful thinking?)
   _____

   Comments:

7. When working on a project, do you stay focused until you complete it? _____

   Comments:

How many always responses did you have on your self-assessment? If you're like most people, there probably is room for improvement. What counts is what you're committed to do to make tomorrow's results better.

The following tool can give you insight into your overall commitments and activities. In fact, when it's complete there will be enough data on the following chart to give you many hours of thought, reflection and decision-making for your priorities, as well as help in answering the questions on the preceding self-assessment.

Key Functions Chart

Key Functions	a. Time Spent	b. Skill Required	c. Personal Satisfaction	d. Results (Personal)	e. Results (Organizational)

STEP ONE: Key Functions. List in the left column the five most important functions of your job, i.e., the five major responsibilities for which you earn your paycheck. Don't try to list them in any particular order — you'll rank them in several ways after the five items are identified.

STEP TWO: Time Spent. Thinking about those five key functions, in column *a* rank them in order based on total amount of time you spend on each function. The function on which you spend the most time is #1. The item you spend the next greatest amount of time on is #2, and so forth down to

5

#5, which will be the item among the five on which you spend the least time.

STEP THREE: Skill Required. Which of the five job functions require the greatest amount of your personal skill and expertise to perform? In column *b*, rank it #1. Rank the others in sequence down to #5, the function which requires the least skill and expertise.

STEP FOUR: Personal Satisfaction. Which function do you enjoy the most, i.e., what gives you the most personal satisfaction in doing? In column *c*, rank it #1. Rank the others in sequence down to #5, the one you like the least.

STEP FIVE: Results. Results should be rated two ways. First, which job function produces the most personal benefit to you? Next, which job function creates the greatest results for your organization? Rank them from 1 to 5 each way. These may be the same, but not necessarily.

Key Function Analysis

If this were an ideal world, every column in your Key Functions Chart would be exactly the same as all the others where the rankings would be identical all the way across the chart. Since you don't live and work in an ideal world, exploration of the implications of your rankings needs to be made.

- If there are any two columns we would want to make certain matched up, we would pick *a* and *d* or *a* and *e*. It just seems logical that a person ought to be spending time on the activities that are going to produce the greatest payoff, be it personal or organizational. If this is not the case, you may want to analyze your time commitments.

- Compare columns *a* and *b*. If the variance between these columns is three or more, decide if the function

5

is necessary. If you're spending the greatest amount of time on a job function that is only #5 in terms of skill required, why are you the one doing it? This function might be delegated to someone else, freeing up your time for activities you have been trained to do.

- Looking at *b* and *c*, if these two columns do match, congratulations! You have just succeeded in turning a *hobby* into a *career*. If, on the other hand, what you like to do and what you do well are not rated similarly, perhaps you might want to consider reevaluating whether you're in the right position.

- If columns *c* and *d* or *c* and *e* do not match, you may very well be headed for burnout. If the activities that are greatest in terms of results and payoff are things you truly don't enjoy, then you are never going to be satisfied. Something must change eventually, and this may be an early warning sign. Research consistently states that you must have at least 20 percent of your day doing what you really enjoy or productivity drops drastically.

A Systematic Approach to Time and Priority Management

Your initial response to these questions gives you a realistic overview. Now, what you need is a system. To start, here are two questions to test the use of your time and priorities. Your answers will help you personalize your own organization system.

> *DON'T AGONIZE.*
> *ORGANIZE AND PERSONALIZE.*

- Is this the best use of my time?
- Is this the right time to be doing it?

To test the use of your time and priorities, and evaluate your answers to the two questions above, here are five specific goals you can set for yourself right now.

Test Your Use of Time and Priorities

WORKSHEET Goal	Target Date	Completion Date
1. I will invest 30 minutes listing the things I am already committed to.		
2. I will invest 15 minutes each day listing the different ways I am presently spending my time.		
3. I will invest 30 minutes reviewing my calendar or appointment book for the past month.		
4. I will invest the time necessary to compare my goals to the actual way I am spending my life and to my present commitments.		
5. I will invest enough time alone to write three short-range goals and three long-range goals for my life.		

Are you willing to commit yourself to these short yet important activities? If so, establish a target date in the appropriate box for completing each of the five goals listed above. When these five goals have been achieved, they will enable you to prioritize your activities from both a practical and a realistic position while taking into account your present lifestyle.

If, from time to time, things are not as you would like them to be, here are some additional tools to help you develop a balanced, realistic action plan.

5

Prioritizing Process Planning

Self-Assessment: Effective-Living Chart

POSSIBLE LIFE AREAS	PRESENTLY COMMITTED	DOING, NOT COMMITTED	TARGETED FOR GOALS
Career/ Occupation			
Employer			
Finances			
Others:			
God			
Spouse			
Children			
Relatives			
Friends			
Business Associates			
Others:			
Education			
Skill			
Advancement			
Community			
Civic			
Hobbies			
Relaxation			
Recreation			
Physical Health			
Emotional Well-Being			
Family			
Education			
Home			
Investment			
Car			
Transportation			
Retirement			
Others:			

5

Directions:

1. Look at the Possible Life Areas column for the items listed. Not all of these areas may apply to you personally.

2. If you are already committed to an item on the list, put an X in the Presently Committed column.

3. If you are involved in something but are not really committed to what you're doing, place the X in the Doing, Not Committed column.

4. Determine in which of these areas you should be setting specific goals by putting an X in the Targeted for Goals column.

NOTE: You may want to do this chart and then share it with others involved in the various activities, noting agreements or disagreements on the areas of commitment or the need to set goals.

"It's not enough that we do our best. Sometimes we have to do what is required."

— Winston Churchill

5

Self-Assessment: Present Commitments Chart

Directions:

Make a list of your present commitments, including personal, family and work commitments. These might include family activities, job responsibilities, finances, hobbies committed to, activities planned with friends, educational classes — anything for which and to which you have made a commitment. Determine which commitments are yours alone, and which are jointly shared by you and other members of your family or work associates. An example is provided:

PRESENT COMMITMENT	WORK	PERSONAL	FAMILY
$100,000 loan to United Mortgage		X	X
Weekly breakfast w/Tom Smith	X		
Community Church trustee board		X	
Weekly dinner out with spouse			X
Annual income tax return		X	
Office collection for cancer fund	X		

PRESENT COMMITMENT	WORK	PERSONAL	FAMILY

Self-Assessment: Your Time Investment

Directions:

To decide if this is the right time to accomplish a task, fill in the chart below. List anything that comes to your mind regarding home, business, family, etc. Include job activities, personal activities, family activities and leisure activities.

Here's a sample Time Investment Chart:

MY TIME-INVESTMENT CHART			
ACTIVITY	ENOUGH	TOO LITTLE	TOO MUCH
• Personal Activities			
Eating		X	
Sleeping	X		

Once again, this chart is only an example.

5

TIME-INVESTMENT CHART—PERSONAL ACTIVITIES			
ACTIVITY	ENOUGH	TOO LITTLE	TOO MUCH
• Personal Activities			
• Job Activities			
• Leisure Activities			
• Family Activities			

When you have completed the list, analyze and evaluate each item. What is your opinion regarding the time investment you make in each activity? Is it enough? Not enough? Too much?

Do a Weekly Time Inventory

To verify the above activities, keep track of everything you do for an entire week, in 30-minute time frames, from the time you get up until you go to bed. Make a real effort to fill this in, every box, every day, for a week.

Why do this? Very few people think about time this much, or follow it this closely. We get used to having one hour just flow into the next, moving from one appointment or activity to another, letting circumstances dictate our pace and schedule. This kind of inventory is the best way to discover what you are really doing with your time, and will help you determine the best choices for how to use your time most effectively. You will probably be surprised at the results! You'll find you're spending much more time on some activities than you imagined, and perhaps a lot less than you think in other areas. That's all the more reason to try it for a week and see for yourself. You'll need at least seven copies of the blank form here to complete a week.

WEEKLY TIME INVENTORY		Day _____		
TIME	**DAY 1**	**DAY 2**	**DAY 3**	**DAY 4**
6:00 am				
6:30 am				
7:00 am				
7:30 am				
8:00 am				
8:30 am				
9:00 am				
9:30 am				
10:00 am				
10:30 am				
11:00 am				
11:30 am				
12 noon				
12:30 pm				
1:00 pm				
1:30 pm				
2:00 pm				
2:30 pm				
3:00 pm				
3:30 pm				
4:00 pm				
4:30 pm				
5:00 pm				
5:30 pm				
6:00 pm				
6:30 pm				
7:00 pm				
7:30 pm				
8:00 pm				
8:30 pm				
9:00 pm				
9:30 pm				
10:00 pm				
10:30 pm				
11:00 pm				

Review Your Appointments and Regularly Scheduled Meetings

The following is a sample page from an appointment book:

Monday	Friday
12:15 Lunch with Tom 7:30 Board Meeting	 7:30 Pizza with kids
Tuesday 7:30 Breakfast with Sam	**Saturday** 8:00 Dinner with Smiths
Wednesday 12:30 Lunch with Betty 2:00 Project presentation	**Sunday** 8:00 Plan for week w/Jonathan
Thursday 8:00 Tennis match	

Self-Assessment: Appointment and Scheduled Meeting Review

Directions:

Refer to your calendar and use the current week, or the most recent typical week if this one was unusual, to complete the chart below. Fill in the chart with all the non-work activities you were involved in for the past week. In addition, note activities performed during regular work hours that are outside your normal scope of responsibilities.

Monday	Friday
Tuesday	**Saturday**
Wednesday	**Sunday**
Thursday	

5

Applying the Inventories — Short-Term

Directions:

Once you've had a chance to complete all the forms up to this point in this chapter, compare the forms with your written goals in Chapter 4. From your seven daily inventory sheets, check off the items that you feel could be associated or identified with specific goals. Put an X beside the items that apparently have nothing to do with your goals.

Then, ask yourself:

1. Did I do things not related to my goals?

2. Which activities were time-wasters that could be eliminated?

3. Are there any "hidden" goals I noticed and want to add to my list?

4. What activities could be reduced, eliminated or delegated?

5. Were these activities I wanted to do, or things someone else wanted me to do?

Applying the Inventories — Long-Term

Directions:

Set aside a week each year and take this inventory again. Make it the same week each year, if possible, or at least around the same time period each year. You might want to use a recurring week that would remind you to do this each year, such as the last week of your organization's fiscal year or the first full week of the calendar year. Expect your goals to change from year to year. It's truly a process. To be effective, you must continually set your goals, review your priorities, make your plans, and then start putting all you've committed to into action.

You will find an improvement in your effectiveness after making a conscious effort at prioritizing. Bad habits will be readily uncovered and can be eliminated before they become too deeply entrenched. Practice using these planning tools — they will give you a great chance of developing beneficial habits.

5

"The chains of habits are too weak to be felt until they are too strong to be broken."

– Samuel Johnson

5

Other very important questions:

- Is there a way I can:
    a. Standardize this?
    b. Delegate this?
    c. Group this with other tasks?

This question represents a real organizing tool.

When doing a task, ask yourself these questions:

- Is this something I've done before? Likely to do again?

- If I could take time now to set up a format I could use over again, would it be a good idea?

- Could I put it in such form that other people could use it, too?

- If it's a written document, is now the time to create once and forever a "boiler-plated" version that could be used many times in the future?

Before you start is the time to decide whether or not the task can be delegated. There's probably no better time than now to teach the process to someone else. The more people who can do anything, the less likely you are to have to do it yourself. In determining whether you should "batch" an activity, decide whether it could be combined with another related project. While you have the materials out, what else requires the same things? For example, if you have to make a trip to the mailroom, what else could you do since you're going to be up and around, anyway?

The A-B-Cs and 1-2-3s of Priorities

Ranking the activities on your daily action or next steps list with the letters A, B and C is a useful step in setting priorities. In considering each item separately, assign a letter priority as follows:

- "A" priority items are the ones that are urgent. They should have been done yesterday. If they're not done soon, big trouble is around the bend. If they have a specific date for a deadline, it's probably today. (Quadrant 1 Crises)

- "B" priority items are still important. They may even have a definite deadline, but these activities are not as critical as the "A" priorities. If one of these items weren't completed today, the world would not come to an end. (Quadrant 2 Importants)

- "C" priority items have no time frame. These may even be small and relatively unimportant (perhaps even potential in-between time activities). Energy and attention need not be devoted to these right now. (Quadrants 3 and 4)

In using the A-B-C priority ranking system, you avoid attempting to assign absolute priorities to your projects and activities. Instead, you divide them into the major categories of A-B-C. For practice, here's a sample list of 15 typical goals you might have. Go through these, using the A-B-C technique, and rank them according to your estimate of their relative importance.

Worksheet: A-B-C Priority Ranking

PERSONAL GOALS	PRIORITY
1. Read one book per week	
2. Maintain membership on only three committees	
3. Invest 15 minutes daily on Action Plan	
4. Invest 15 minutes daily in inspiration (spiritual, etc.)	
5. Take a class on how to get along with difficult people	
6. Learn to fly an airplane by the end of next summer	
7. Take 10 tennis lessons in the next six months	
8. Compliment at least one person per day	
9. Make contact with a manager from a competitor company	
10. Reorganize work area by the end of the month	
11. Buy a personal calendar and appointment book	
12. Increase daily exercise to lose five pounds next month	
13. Take family members to a favorite restaurant this month	
14. Spend 15 quality minutes daily with my "significant other"	
15. Write a Slight-Edge idea to practice each week	

It's sometimes a good idea to watch the "C" priorities for a while to see what happens to them. Things don't tend to stay at "C" level. These activities either move up the chart to a higher ranking, or they drop off the list completely because they resolved themselves. Someone else did them or they never really needed to be done.

There are some activities that don't merit a ranking at all. Remember, just because an activity has been presented to you to complete doesn't mean you're obligated to do it. If something is a complete waste of time, keep it off of your priority chart.

Now that you've had some practice with a sample listing of activities, look at the next chart. Photocopy the chart before you begin writing, so it can be used over and over. First, put your daily action list on the chart; write in each project or activity you plan to do for the day. Then, consider each item on the list based on the prioritization criteria discussed above and rank each item A, B or C.

5

5

Worksheet: Personal A-B-C Priority Ranking

DAILY ACTION LIST	PRIORITY
1.	
2.	
3.	
4.	
5.	
6.	
7.	
8.	
9.	
10.	
11.	
12.	
13.	
14.	
15.	

Your daily action list just became more useful, because now you have separated the items into categories of importance. This will help your decision-making throughout the day because you recognize what you're doing, and what its relative importance is.

Unfortunately, the A-B-C prioritizing system does not tell you what task to do in what order. If you have 15 items, there might be five As, five Bs and five Cs. Since you can only do one thing at a time, if five items have the same importance, which do you do first?

Here's where the numbering system comes in. If you do have five "A" priority items on your list, consider only those five items. Which one is most important? Even if they are all critically important, you can only do one at a time, so you must choose which it will be. When you've determined which one it is, this becomes your A-1 item.

If there are still more tasks left, choose again: Which is the next most important item? That becomes A-2. Continue to rank these until you have assigned a numerical order to all your "A" priority items. Do the same thing for the "B" and "C" priority items on your list. But don't delay doing A-1 by taking your time ranking the Bs and Cs. When you've done this for all items, rewrite your daily action list, this time putting each item in ranked order of importance (A-1, A-2, A-3, B-1, B-2, etc.).

Many other factors, including common sense, enter into play here. It is poor management to become a slave to a list! The best list still just gives you information you can assess to draw the right conclusions about what to do, and why.

It's not too soon to impress upon you the most important thought concerning all ranking and priorities: You stay in control. Not someone else and certainly not the list.

ANY PRIORITY LISTING IS ONLY A GUIDE IN HELPING ME MAKE THE RIGHT DECISIONS.

For example, there's a phone call on your daily action list. It's short, and may take only 10 minutes. It's not the A-1 item on the list. But, if the only time of day your party will be available is between 8:30 and 9:00 this morning, when should you make the call?

Any item on your list is subject to all sorts of other factors besides an absolute-priority ranking. Time, conditions and circumstances all are part of the decisions. But if you don't know the priority of an item, it's easy to make the wrong choice. That's why the ranking has to come first.

> *THE DIFFERENCE BETWEEN SAGES AND FOOLS IS THEIR CHOICE AND USE OF THEIR TOOLS.*

Priority Indicator

Naturally, you're going to have some days when everything is a top priority — when you believe you couldn't possibly choose one task over another as more important, or when you've started on the most important task of the day, then something more important comes up.

Obviously, you can't do 10 things at once. You must be focused and directed. An excellent way to focus your energy and thinking involves using a priority indicator. This "forced-choice" indicator compels you to choose between options. What's nice about it is that no matter how many items are being considered, the choice is only between two items at a time.

A priority indicator has two parts: On the left, there's a series of numbered blanks. This tool can be used with as few as three items to a virtually unlimited number. All the items from the list go in these blanks, in no particular order (that's what the tool itself will determine). On the right, there is a series of numbers, ever increasing in size. The numbers are considered in groups of two — the one number over the other in each case.

Looking at the illustration below, suppose you did have five items on your list, and each one seemed to be A-1 in importance:

- A report that was due yesterday
- A phone call to a client who is very unhappy about something
- Planning and developing a departmental budget for the upcoming year
- Developing a marketing letter concerning a new product to accompany your mailing list
- Monthly receipts to be posted and deposited

Priority Indicator

Topic	Scale			
1. Report				
2. Phone Call	①			
	2			
3. Budget	①	2		
	3	③		
4. Marketing Letter	1	2	3	
	④	④	④	
5. Receipts	1	2	3	④
	⑤	⑤	⑤	5

My A-1 priority for tomorrow is **Marketing Letter**

The five items are listed in the illustration and numbered in the same sequence as described. The circled numbers in the example correspond to the following choices.

First, there is no group of numbers next to #1. You can't compare something with itself! Next to #2, the numbers 1 over 2 tell us to compare only #1 and #2 with each other. Don't worry about anything else on the list. Just ask yourself which is more important: 1 or 2? Circle the number you chose. In the example, we chose #1, the report, over #2, the phone call.

Then, move on to #3. This time there are two sets of numbers off to the right, because now you have two choices. You will compare #1 with #3 and choose which one is more important, then compare #2 with #3, again circling your choice in each instance. We chose #1 when we compared it to #3, and selected #3 when we compared it to #2. Next to #4 are three sets of numbers: 1 and 4, 2 and 4, 3 and 4. Make each comparison and circle your selections. You can see our choices in the illustration.

Next to #5 are four sets of numbers, because you must compare this new item with everything else already on the list. After you've made these four choices by circling, the selection is finished.

The final step, once all choices have been made, is to go back and count how many times you circled each number on the right-hand side and write that total on the lines to the left of each number. The one you circled most often (in this case, four times) is your true #1 priority item. The remaining items can be ranked in priority order based on frequency of selection, and the one you chose the least times (none) is last on the list. In our illustration, we determined, by counting how many times we circled each selection, that the marketing letter was the most important of the five activities we compared.

This doesn't necessarily mean the #1 priority item is the one you're going to work on first! Don't forget, any ranking like this is only meant to be used as a guide. Other outside factors and your own common sense will help you answer, what the best use of your time is right now.

5

Worksheet: The Priority Indicator — Practice (blank)

1. _____ _____

2. _____ _____ $\frac{1}{2}$

3. _____ _____ $\frac{1}{3}$ $\frac{2}{3}$

4. _____ _____ $\frac{1}{4}$ $\frac{2}{4}$ $\frac{3}{4}$

5. _____ _____ $\frac{1}{5}$ $\frac{2}{5}$ $\frac{3}{5}$ $\frac{4}{5}$

6. _____ _____ $\frac{1}{6}$ $\frac{2}{6}$ $\frac{3}{6}$ $\frac{4}{6}$ $\frac{5}{6}$

7. _____ _____ $\frac{1}{7}$ $\frac{2}{7}$ $\frac{3}{7}$ $\frac{4}{7}$ $\frac{5}{7}$ $\frac{6}{7}$

8. _____ _____ $\frac{1}{8}$ $\frac{2}{8}$ $\frac{3}{8}$ $\frac{4}{8}$ $\frac{5}{8}$ $\frac{6}{8}$ $\frac{7}{8}$

9. _____ _____ $\frac{1}{9}$ $\frac{2}{9}$ $\frac{3}{9}$ $\frac{4}{9}$ $\frac{5}{9}$ $\frac{6}{9}$ $\frac{7}{9}$ $\frac{8}{9}$

10. _____ _____ $\frac{1}{10}$ $\frac{2}{10}$ $\frac{3}{10}$ $\frac{4}{10}$ $\frac{5}{10}$ $\frac{6}{10}$ $\frac{7}{10}$ $\frac{8}{10}$ $\frac{9}{10}$

11. _____ _____ $\frac{1}{11}$ $\frac{2}{11}$ $\frac{3}{11}$ $\frac{4}{11}$ $\frac{5}{11}$ $\frac{6}{11}$ $\frac{7}{11}$ $\frac{8}{11}$ $\frac{9}{11}$ $\frac{10}{11}$

12. _____ _____ $\frac{1}{12}$ $\frac{2}{12}$ $\frac{3}{12}$ $\frac{4}{12}$ $\frac{5}{12}$ $\frac{6}{12}$ $\frac{7}{12}$ $\frac{8}{12}$ $\frac{9}{12}$ $\frac{10}{12}$ $\frac{11}{12}$

13. _____ _____ $\frac{1}{13}$ $\frac{2}{13}$ $\frac{3}{13}$ $\frac{4}{13}$ $\frac{5}{13}$ $\frac{6}{13}$ $\frac{7}{13}$ $\frac{8}{13}$ $\frac{9}{13}$ $\frac{10}{13}$ $\frac{11}{13}$ $\frac{12}{13}$

14. _____ _____ $\frac{1}{14}$ $\frac{2}{14}$ $\frac{3}{14}$ $\frac{4}{14}$ $\frac{5}{14}$ $\frac{6}{14}$ $\frac{7}{14}$ $\frac{8}{14}$ $\frac{9}{14}$ $\frac{10}{14}$ $\frac{11}{14}$ $\frac{12}{14}$ $\frac{13}{14}$

15. _____ _____ $\frac{1}{15}$ $\frac{2}{15}$ $\frac{3}{15}$ $\frac{4}{15}$ $\frac{5}{15}$ $\frac{6}{15}$ $\frac{7}{15}$ $\frac{8}{15}$ $\frac{9}{15}$ $\frac{10}{15}$ $\frac{11}{15}$ $\frac{12}{15}$ $\frac{13}{15}$ $\frac{14}{15}$

If you've completed your practice worksheet, you probably now know that it is still possible for more than one item to be ranked in the same priority. So what should you do? No problem, really. It may be final proof that two or more items are truly equal in importance, and the choice is yours as to how to list them. The longer the list of items you compare, the more likely you are to have some ties.

Another factor you've probably been wondering about is the number of items that can realistically be compared. The form shows room for 20 items. Obviously, the more items you try to compare at once, the longer your list of numbers and the more choices you'll have to make. If your lists exceeds 20 items, divide in half and complete two priority indicators. Then mesh the two rankings together.

The priority indicator is most helpful when prioritizing items that are unrelated. This is called an absolute priority because one item is in no way dependent on another. Another kind of prioritizing is called time or sequential priority, which is really more a scheduling technique than a prioritization tool. In time priority, ranking items isn't necessary because the calendar does it for you; e.g., you'll have your 10 a.m. appointment before the 2 p.m. meeting.

In sequential priority, things have to be done in a particular sequence because they are dependent on each other. In construction, you must pour the foundation before you shingle the roof. One is not more important than the other, but one definitely comes first in the sequence, and your ability to complete one activity is dependent on the completion of the other. The priority indicator isn't appropriate for this kind of prioritizing; this is when a PERT or GANTT chart is actually a more useful tool (see Chapter 10). Information from these tools can also help you establish the most productive work day possible.

Remember, any ranking of priorities is done to give you control over your activities, not vice versa. And the role of common sense in producing good judgment cannot be overstated. These tools will be helpful any time you need to communicate your priorities to someone else, and can even help you say no to someone when your priorities have been established.

5

Work Action Plan

The following Work Action Plan chart is one you'll want to photocopy and use daily — you may even choose to use the chart when making your Daily Action Plan. There's room to list the activities of the day (see separate categories) and rank them, first by A-B-C, then by 1-2-3. A nice feature of the chart are the check-off boxes that allow you to check off the items as you complete them.

The Best Time column can also be used in a number of ways: (1) you can list the energy levels — high, medium or low — required to do each task and perform it according to your energy curves; (2) you can assign specific times of day to each item (like the phone call in the illustration); or (3) you can estimate how long each activity should require to ensure a realistic daily action list.

WORK ACTION PLAN				
ACTIVITY	RANK		BEST TIME	COMPLETED ✔
	A, B, C...	1, 2, 3...		

Summary of Key Points

- Making a commitment to do something, rather than just trying to do something, is the key to accomplishing what you want.

- Applying the 80-20 Rule to priorities, you can be 80 percent successful by achieving only 20 percent of your goals.

- To be productive, work on things in ranked priority order.

- Considering the numbers in the Key Functions chart will give you many insights into yourself and where you put your energy at work.

- Getting things done first means making a commitment to plan, organize and prioritize.

- By comparing what you actually do with the goals you have set, you can determine if your energy is pointed in the right direction.

- Recording and studying your activities for a period of time can be very insightful in showing your effectiveness, or lack of it.

- Look for ways to standardize, delegate or batch regular activities for better organization and control.

- Ranking your priorities will help you in decision-making throughout the day, as well as help you determine the most productive use of your time at any given moment.

- Never surrender control to your priority list. It's only a guide.

- Two great habits of self-management are finishing the things you start and handling a thing only one time.

- Doing a forced-choice priority indicator will provide you with an absolute priority ranking.

- If your boss is in love with a project, you'd better be too.

- If you've never done something before, its unknown characteristics make it top priority.

- Put any project with high visibility (and high risk) at the top of your list.

- Remember the needs of your customers, peers and subordinates when ranking the activities on your own list.

Putting Priorities to Work in Your Life

1. How can you be 80 percent effective on your job?

2. What were the two most important insights you gained from the Key Functions chart? How are you going to apply those insights? When?

3. Have you committed yourself to goals for analyzing your activities and time usage for greater future productivity?

4. What personal activities did you determine you were spending too little time doing? Too much time?

5. When are you going to do your Weekly Time Inventory?

6. What are some activities on your job you could standardize? Delegate? Batch?

7. What is your A-1 project for tomorrow?

8. Will you commit yourself to applying the charts in this chapter until their daily completion becomes a habit? When will you begin?

9. Chart a 30-day course of action. Reassess your progress in 30 days and modify your plan.

5

> *Action TNT — Today Not Tomorrow*
>
> *No one ever built a reputation based on what they were going to do tomorrow.*

MY SLIGHT-EDGE IDEAS
ABOUT SETTING PRIORITIES:

5

5

*C*HAPTER 6

Overcoming Overcommitment

"Besides the noble art of getting things done, there is the noble art of leaving things undone."

Lin Yu Tang, Oriental Philosopher

Most people are chronically overcommitted. They stay on the run, busily trying to accomplish a plethora of tasks, most of which are not even particularly important to them. The question, "Why am I doing this?" is frequently asked, followed shortly by "I wish I had just said NO."

NO. What a powerful word! It's very positive. It's easy to pronounce and no one ever misspells it. It's pronounced the same, or nearly so, in many other languages. It can make the difference between success and failure. It can free us from stress and pressure. It can give us control of our lives. Yet this little word is not used often enough. People avoid it at all costs, and often the cost is very high indeed. The result? Ineffective performance, spiritless effort and utter frustration.

How do you know if you are overcommitted? That's easy. If you feel like you are, you are. Whether you've already reached the breaking point or see the point approaching fast, to avoid certain demise you must take a long, hard look at all of your commitments and activities. The best organized schedule, the most well-planned Daily Action List, the most effectively applied list of "10 steps" or "12 ideas" cannot change your situation if you are simply trying to accomplish more than you have time to do. You must be honest; and you must be realistic. You deceive everyone including yourself by acting as if the conditions didn't exist.

Just how badly overcommitted are you? See for yourself.

Assessment: Overcommitted?

Check yourself on these questions to see how overloaded you may be. Read the statements and circle the number that best describes your response.

	Agree	Unsure	Disagree
1. I feel totally responsible for the completion of group projects.	3	2	1
2. I believe the job is always done best if I do it myself.	3	2	1
3. I am unable to satisfy my family's needs and requests.	3	2	1
4. I am involved in many things I wish I could get out of	3	2	1
5. I feel guilty because I can't devote enough time to some things.	3	2	1
6. Any time I join a group, I take a leadership position.	3	2	1
7. I am so busy I don't have time to eat, sleep or relax.	3	2	1
8. I have trouble deciding what's really important vs what's urgent.	3	2	1
9. I seldom say "no" when I'm asked to do something.	3	2	1
10. I don't want to let anybody down, so I usually agree to help.	3	2	1

6

Interpretation:

In this assessment, a high score is bad, not good.

24 or more: You're on a collision course with disaster

23-15: You deserve more of yourself than you're getting

less than 15: Congratulations! You're in control for now

Overcommitment and Stress

The total absence of stress is death. An extreme overload of stress is death. The key is finding the middle ground between the two. Studies have indicated that a certain degree of stress is essential for motivation and top performance but too much rapidly destroys both the performance and the performer.

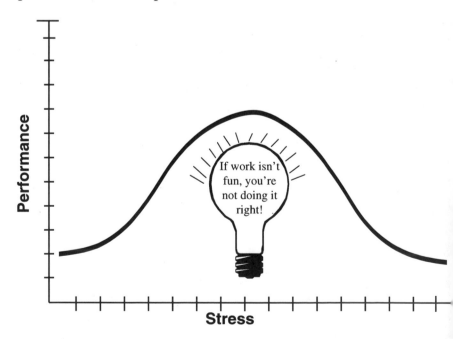

Many factors contribute to stress overload. The perpetual push to perform, to overcome life's setbacks and disappointments, and to meet everyone's expectations has become a heavy burden for many.

Life's stressors are a combination of fate and choice. Therefore, managing your choices is critical to your continued health and well-being. *You must choose to overcome your habit of overcommitting yourself.*

Five Steps for Overcoming Overcommitment:

1. Make a list of *everything* you are committed to do. Make a separate list for professional and personal activities

2. Make a list of everything you should be and really want to be doing but are not.

3. Review the lists from #1. Based on the time you have available and your own priorities, which of these things should you not be doing?

4. Make a plan to extricate yourself from all items identified in #3.

5. Specify when you will begin each of the items identified in #2.

Reducing your commitment load is critical to your success and well-being. A closer examination of each of these critical steps is warranted.

Step 1: Make a list of everything you are committed to do. Everything means everything, no matter what.

Step 2: Make a list of everything you should or really want to be doing but are not. Failing to do things you really need and/or feel you should be doing is one of the fastest ways to raise your guilt threshold, burn yourself out, and diminish your effectiveness in all other areas. Answer these questions:

a. What is really important to you? What are your priorities?

b. What do you wish you had more time and energy to pursue but simply can't because of other commitments? Be specific and don't hold back. You may not be able to get to all of them anytime soon, but they still must be identified to ease your mind.

Step 3: Review the lists from #1. Based on the time you have available and your own priorities, which of these things should you not be doing? Assess each item as follows:

a. Is this important to you? Does it fit into your Quadrant 2 definition of important?

b. If you were not already doing this, would you choose to get involved? Hindsight is always clearer than foresight! Have you ever said, "If I had only known then what I know now, I would never have gotten involved"? These are the first activities to be eliminated.

c. Must you personally do this? Can and should you make a strong personal commitment to invest your time and abilities in this purpose, project or pursuit? If the answer is no, then it's best not to start it, or if already involved, find a way out.

> *DEVOTING A LITTLE OF YOURSELF TO EVERYTHING MEANS COMMITTING A GREAT DEAL OF YOURSELF TO NOTHING.*

Step 4. Make a plan to extricate yourself from the items identified in #3.

Removing yourself from a previous commitment is sometimes difficult but necessary. Evaluate each situation. How can you gracefully (or even not so gracefully) take that item off your plate?

If this is a work-related task, and you have a supervisory or management-level position, there is probably someone in your department who is ready to assume a little more authority and responsibility. Pass this task on to them. (See Chapter 9 for some specifics on how to delegate.) Not only does it give this individual the chance to grow and develop skills, it will make you more effective as a manager. A good manager never tries to do it all because it's just not possible.

What if you're not in management and you have no one to delegate to? You're the someone else who is always given that opportunity to grow? Your boss won't let you delegate? Don't give up hope yet. Chapter 10 will discuss ways you can establish and track priorities and negotiate changes in expectations that can allow the release of certain responsibilities.

Everyone can practice delegation with commitments we have made outside work. Have you been the secretary of your bowling league for years? Have you been a leader in a certain club or organization since you started? Are people counting on you to head up the school carnival again? Are you so busy after working hours that your family and friends never see you?

Review all of your commitments. Is it time to step aside for a while and let other people develop some of their leadership potential and try some of their ideas? Could you remove your name from the ballot this time around? Could you bring someone in to help you in an official capacity that would make your life easier? Do you have a vice president who doesn't really do anything? Would that organization continue without your involvement? Is it actually more important to you than to anybody else?

Would you feel a tremendous burden was lifted off your shoulders if people didn't depend on you for this any longer? If you're answering yes, then delegate. Don't let a do-it-myself attitude dilute your effectiveness.

Step 5: Specify when you will begin each of the items identified in #2. These "should be doing but are not" items must be worked into your schedule. They are what you need and want to be doing based on your own priorities and values. These are the items that will allow you to be fulfilled and meet your own needs and desires.

Make yourself a plan. Make a commitment to it. Then do it.

> *ALL YOU CAN DO IS ALL YOU CAN DO ...*
> *AND ALL YOU CAN DO IS ENOUGH.*

Avoiding a Repeat Performance

While you are implementing your plan, you'll need to also develop the awareness and skill to keep other activities from creeping into your life. Once you have opened the door to them, even just a crack, they are likely to walk in and take over.

In short, you must learn to assess each new request realistically before agreeing to take it on.

- **Listen closely.** This in itself is a lost art. Don't just hear the words, but get a clear picture of what is being asked — what it is and what it involves. Ask questions if you're not certain. The more thoroughly you understand what someone is asking you to do, the better your response can be. Don't distract your concentration to think about what you will say. You're entitled to take a minute to think about that before you have to respond. Listening is a very positive step because it gives mutual respect both to the speaker and to you, the listener.

- **Stop. Pause. And think.** Humans have an almost deathly fear of silence. Learn the art of quiet contemplation, and use it after a request has been given. Control your impulse to speak. This is your opportunity to consider what has been said and, even more importantly, to consider what you're going to say in reply. Ask yourself, "Do I really want to do this?" and "Can I realistically do it, give it the time it deserves without burning myself out?"

  Remember the last time someone told you about a new organization or a new activity, and as that person described it, it sounded so interesting? Couldn't you almost already see yourself involved? Before jumping in with both feet, take a hard, realistic look at your schedule and ask exactly where and how you

6

intend to schedule this into your life. Evaluate how much time it will take and multiply that by 1.25.

— If you think a meeting will take one hour, allow one hour and 15 minutes on your schedule.

— If you think it will take four hours to prepare a presentation, schedule five hours.

— If the committee meets once a week, plan on five times a month.

— If the task is totally unfamiliar to you, estimate the time and multiply by 1.5 instead of 1.25.

Schedule only 50 percent of your time. Already 100 percent booked? You're not alone. Since most of us have already filled nearly all of our allotted time, in order to add a new activity, something has to move out. Are you prepared to do that? What activity would that be? Better yet, what really is most important to you — your true priority? This is the time to recommit yourself to what you really believe is important, and direct unscheduled time in that direction before adding something else.

These services should remain unscheduled:

1. All low-priority items unless the high-priority items have been completed.

2. Any task that when completed is of little or no consequence.

3. Anything you can delegate to someone else. Consider household repairs and improvements. You may immerse yourself in a project only to find that you don't have the time, training or tools to successfully complete it. You may even complicate the problem. You run the high risk of pouring your time and energy into a bottomless pit and ending up empty-handed.

4. Anything done just to please others because you fear their displeasure or want them to be indebted to you.

5. Thoughtless or inappropriate requests for your time and effort. Think about this one. Aren't there people constantly trying to do this to you?

6. Anything others should be doing for themselves.

• **Evaluate your priorities.** What will you have to give up doing in order to do this? The most difficult choices are not between those things you want to do and those you do not. The hard choices are between two or more things you are truly interested in. Each choice will have an impact on all your other priorities. Be sure to weigh each opportunity in terms of what your alternative time commitment might be. For example, suppose you are actively involved in a particular civic or charity group that is very important to you. A critical meeting has been scheduled for a specific evening. At the last minute, professional opportunity arises for you to meet some very influential people in your field ... but it is on the same night as your previously planned meeting. What do you do? You want to do both but that is impossible. You must weigh the options and choose the one you need/want to pursue the most. There are no right or wrong answers. Only ones that are true to your own situation and priorities.

• **Decide immediately.** Once you've determined you are going to decline, tell your listener: "I'm going to have to say NO." Then pause and control your impulse to continue talking. That's it. Such an easy statement can save so much time and energy. But when it gets to that point, most of us chicken out. Instead we say:

> ## *"I WANT TO THINK ABOUT IT!"*

or

> ## *"LET ME GET BACK TO YOU ON THIS."*

or

> ## *"MAYBE."*

Sound familiar? That classic noncommittal answer gets you ultimately committed. Inside, you're kicking yourself. You don't want to do it. Your stomach is tied up in knots. The longer you wait, the more you are likely to replay it in your mind, wasting valuable mental and sometimes physical energy. Just say no quickly, decisively and pleasantly.

Many of us just don't know how to refuse a request placed against our time. So we say yes for two very negative reasons: We are afraid someone else will have a lesser opinion of us, or a request for our help indulges our own egos by giving us a false sense of importance and power.

When you say yes because of a need for approval, you are saying that someone else's opinion of you is more important than your opinion of yourself. Saying yes to feel important is the ammunition of martyrs and victims, not the essence of leadership!

Shortly after Norman Vincent Peale published his best-selling book, *The Power of Positive Thinking*, he suddenly was in great demand as a speaker. From all over the country, offers poured onto his desk at

Marble Collegiate Church in New York. He had many more opportunities than he could possibly fill, even if he had actually wanted to, which he didn't. But no was a hard word for Peale to say, too, and he found himself putting the requests off. He didn't accept them, but he didn't turn them down. Only after his delays had put the organizations who had asked him in such a bind that the only fair and honorable thing to do was to accept did Peale realize: "It was much easier to say 'no' in the beginning than to end up doing something I didn't want to do in the first place."

Sounds like Dr. Peale also learned that overcommitment inevitably leads to procrastination and even, quite possibly, to failure. *Saying yes to everything decreases the chances of successfully completing even one thing.*

One of the reasons you dislike saying no is you don't want to let somebody else down. To get a clear perspective on things, let's reverse the positions for a moment. If you were going to ask somebody to do something for you, wouldn't you expect to hear no a few times? You probably even make a list of several potential prospects for this job so that if the first one declines, you still have others you can turn to.

Yet when somebody asks you, the tendency is to think your answer is going to make or break the situation for that person. Why wouldn't that person have other names on a list, just like you would? Rarely, if ever, are you somebody else's last resort or only option. That person is expecting that you may say no. And, if you truly are their last resort, then it may well be an inappropriate request of your time and effort. Even if you are last, it still doesn't have to be your problem unless you choose to make it so! In

6

fact, if everyone else has declined doing the task, there may very well be a good reason for their reluctance. The task may just be too time-consuming or just not worthwhile enough to pursue.

- **Have reasons for saying no.** The *reason* for saying no is most valuable to you, as a way of reinforcing what is important. You need to know your reasons to help you maintain your position if the other person tries to persuade you otherwise. If you think it would be beneficial for the other person to know your reasons so they have a better understanding of the situation, fine. Tell them. If you don't want to give your reasons, or believe that it would be better if you just kept your reasons to yourself, a simple no is sufficient. You are under no obligation to explain. Your reasons are really none of the other person's business. If that is too uncomfortable for you to do, you might try following your no with a non-specific reason such as, "My other commitments simply will not allow me to." You'll be surprised how easy saying no becomes with a little practice.

- **Offer alternatives.** Is there another way to do this job that doesn't involve you? Are there other people who might be better able to provide the service you've been asked to handle? Could you offer a counterproposal if you think the request is valid? "I can't sit in for you at the meeting this afternoon, but I'll be happy to answer your phone while you're gone."

Could you possibly suggest an alternative that would allow you to help without taking on such a major time commitment yourself? For example, perhaps someone has just asked you to head the company picnic next summer. There's no way you have the time and energy for a job as big as that. You know you simply can't do the job. So, why not say, "I'm honored to think you would trust me with such a big job, but I'm going to have to say no. However, please tell the person who takes this responsibility I'd be glad to serve on the entertainment committee."

In 1968, newly elected President Richard Nixon asked Art Linkletter to serve the United States as ambassador to Australia. Linkletter had traveled extensively in Australia and owned property there, but he couldn't see himself in the cocktail parties and political rituals of a job in which he wouldn't have any power, but merely serve as a front for Washington. He also knew you couldn't turn the President down flat.

He said, "Mr. President, what would you rather have me do: Go and be our representative in Australia, or attempt to save thousands of young people from the ravages of drug abuse in this country? I have lectures, films, books and fund-raising activities scheduled for this next year. I believe I'm more effective outside the government, so why not just put me on a commission to fight drugs?"

The President agreed. How could he say anything negative about the efforts to fight the drug problem? Linkletter later wrote: "Being an ambassador didn't fit in with my goals, and no was the only answer I could give Richard Nixon. But the way I did it points up something important about the method of turning an offer down. It's not always necessary to give a direct negative answer. There are many ways of saying no without actually saying it. In this encounter with Nixon, I merely offered him another choice, which I knew he would accept."

It all comes down to this:

WHEN I KNOW WHAT'S IMPORTANT TO ME, IT'S EASY TO SAY "NO" TO SOMETHING ELSE.

Making It Work

CONCERN	REASON	STRATEGY
frustration with group or activity	it was more than you thought it would be	begin taking steps now to back out of this job
not enough time to do really important things	too involved in low-priority projects and activities	reconsider priorities: commit yourself to them
too large a share of the responsibility	trying to do it all	identify tasks for immediate delegation to others
no time for something you really want to do	too much time taken up by other projects	let something out to make room for your new activity
inability to say no	don't know how	learn and apply the five steps in this chapter
often get roped into jobs you don't want to do	forced into situation where only answer is yes	decide immediately and say no
pressure to agree to a request for help	don't want to let someone else down	offer alternatives, realize you're not the only hope

Case Study: More Than He Bargained For

Jim North, a personnel director for a small manufacturing firm, began attending meetings of a local organization of personnel directors. The group meets monthly for breakfast and sponsors an annual all-day workshop on a Saturday.

Although Jim enjoyed the association with other professionals in his field, he found it difficult to attend the breakfasts every month. He frequently got his most productive work done early in the day, and sometimes the meetings seemed to have only marginal professional benefits, since a number of the members had known each other for years and seemed mainly interested in the meeting as a social occasion.

Jim was surprised when Gerry Duckworth, a member he knew only casually, called one day and asked if he would consider running for vice president of the organization for the upcoming year. When Jim asked what the position involved, Gerry said, "Oh, you really don't have to do anything. We just need someone to hold that office since our charter calls for it."

Jim told himself he should know better, but agreed to have his name placed in nomination. As it turned out, his was the only name in nomination, and he was elected to the office.

A few days later Kathy Cornell, the president, called Jim and told him there was a lunch meeting scheduled later that week for all the officers of the organization. Jim thought, "An officers' meeting sounds like doing something. But, since I'm vice president, I'll attend."

When Jim went to the officers' meeting, he discovered that the vice president had numerous responsibilities, including planning the programs for the breakfasts each month and heading up the annual new-members campaign.

Kathy excitedly told the group she had just learned her corporation was sending her across the country for three months to oversee the opening of a new office. This meant Jim would function as president for that time, as well.

Suddenly Jim realized, "This job's a lot bigger than I was told it was. If I had known I would have this much responsibility, I would not have agreed to serve as vice president." Jim began to envision the additional hours and energy required (which he really didn't have) to serve an organization of questionable value to him, and felt overwhelmed. He also found himself feeling resentful that the importance of the job had been misrepresented to him.

Questions

1. What was Jim's biggest mistake?

2. If you were Jim North, what would you do?

What Actually Happened

Jim quickly reassessed his own priorities, and determined this new responsibility didn't fit into them. He analyzed what impact giving up that much additional time and energy would have on the activities he had already committed to. He wondered how much more he could do in those areas if he were to direct the same time and energy to his priorities.

At the end of the meeting, he asked Kathy to stay for a few minutes. Jim said, "Kathy, if I had realized the scope of the vice president's job in this association, I would never have agreed to serve. I'm sorry I didn't ask more questions when Gerry called, and I realize this will put the association in a temporary bind, but I'm going to have to resign from the office."

Kathy reluctantly accepted Jim's resignation, but thanked him for his candor and honesty at the beginning, rather than agreeing to handle the responsibility and then not doing the

6

6

job. She appointed another vice president before the next meeting and made the announcement in the chapter's newsletter.

For a few months, Jim felt a little uncomfortable at the meetings. A few people teased him about "chickening out" of the job, but the teasing stopped. When the election of officers came around next year, Jim reflected gratefully on his decision, realizing he had been wise to put his efforts into his priorities.

Analysis

Jim could have decided to make the best of his position and plan great programs and spearhead an enthusiastic member campaign. Maybe he would have even gotten more out of the meetings and his opportunities to network with the other members of the chapter.

But sometimes people simply spread themselves too thin in trying to do too much and please too many people. When you identify your priorities by asking "What's important to me?" it is often far more satisfying and rewarding to redirect additional time and effort to previous commitments than to add even more activities to an already jammed calendar.

Summary of Key Points

- If you feel you are trying to do too much, you are.
- If, knowing what you now know, you would not have gotten involved in an activity, begin to look for ways to drop it.
- Remember: Your first obligation is to look out for yourself, your interests and your priorities. No one will do this for you.
- Develop the habit of asking, "Do I personally have to do this?"

- Follow the Five Steps to Overcoming Overcommitment.

- Take a serious look at your schedule before agreeing to accept new work or responsibilities. If someone won't wait, say no immediately.

- In planning, always allow about 25 percent more time than you think you'll need for getting things done.

- If you can afford to give someone else the job, do it!

- Be alert to the changes in your life. Recognize this as part of growth, and make room for the new activities that arise.

- Practice saying the word no. Have a friend or spouse help you by asking you for things it's easy to say no to.

- Use the power of silence after you've been asked to do something.

- If your ultimate intention is to say no to a request, turn it down immediately. This is a favor to the asker as well as to you.

- Be ready with alternative suggestions; they keep you from feeling as guilty when you have to say no.

Putting Overcoming Overcommitment to Work in Your Life

1. Identify a situation of your own similar to Jim's. Wouldn't you really rather be out from under this responsibility than trying to juggle it and fit it in with other more important matters? Won't it feel good when that commitment is no longer on your list? The benefits you'll get from relieving yourself of burdensome, unnecessary tasks will undoubtedly outweigh the consequences.

6

State the first two steps you need to undertake to relieve yourself of this responsibility and the dates upon which you will pursue them.

2. Ask yourself these questions to determine why you take on too many responsibilities:

   a. Is your impatience leading to overcommitment?

   b. Are you afraid someone else won't do it well enough?

   c. Why do you let other people dump their problems on you?

   d. What is the worst that can happen if you don't take on a project? Can you handle that?

   e. Who are you trying to impress?

   f. Who are you trying to rescue?

3. On what date will you begin the Five Step Process to Overcome Overcommitment?

4. Chart a 30-day course of action. Reassess your progress in 30 days and modify your plan.

6

> ### *Action TNT — Today Not Tomorrow*
> *No one ever built a reputation based on what they were going to do tomorrow.*

6

MY SLIGHT-EDGE IDEAS
FOR OVERCOMING OVERCOMMITMENT:

*C*HAPTER 7

The Deadly Four: Paper, E-mail, Indecision and Procrastination

"The hardest work in the world is that which should have been done yesterday."

Unknown

Paramount to your success is your ability to handle the avalanche of paper and e-mail headed your way, the ability to make decisions quickly and accurately, and the self-discipline to do what needs to be done now.

The Paper Blizzard

Thanks to outstanding technology, paper is being created in phenomenal quantities. In a world where documentation is everything, we are afraid to throw anything away. As a result, filing systems are bursting from the pressure of billions and billions of documents, many of which could never be found even if someone wanted to! It is estimated that 75 to 80 percent of the contents of today's business files are being saved unnecessarily.

The way you control the flow of paper in and out of your office and the decisions you make regarding its retention can make or break your productivity. Many desks today are absolutely buried in paper ... things to do, items waiting for more information, items we have no idea what to do with, the last several weeks of filing, and who knows what else. Most in-boxes have become holding tanks and trash cans have become empty bins. Many are losing the battle, despite being told, "If there's a way to get it on your desk, there's a way to get it off."

The key to paper control is to keep most papers from ever reaching your desk at all.

1. Move your in-box off your desk and outside your office door. If outside the door is not an option, put it just inside. If that's not possible, at least get it out of your line of sight. When you keep your in-box on your desk, several unproductive things happen.

   - The in-box becomes a combination in-box and pending tank.

   - You stop to see what the "incoming" is every time something arrives, interrupting your concentration and focus on the issues currently being pursued.

   - You lose time chatting with the person delivering the new paper.

   Specify a time or times during the day that you will devote to reviewing and dispatching the contents of your in-box.

2. With the in-box should be a filing receptacle, a waste basket, inner-office envelopes, and an out-box.

3. Decide at what interval(s) during the day you will check the in-box. Is once a day sufficient? Twice daily? Hourly?

4. Whatever you decide, stick with your schedule and stay away from your in-box at other times.

5. At the designated time, go to your in-box. Do NOT bring it to your desk. Review the contents of the box while standing.

- Those items that are simply FYI and need to be retained, skim and place with papers to be filed.

- For those items that should be handled by someone else, jot a note on the item if necessary, complete the inner-office envelope and place it directly in your out-box.

- Meeting arrangements and schedules should be noted on your calendar and the notice thrown away. If a meeting agenda is included, place it in your tickler file (details to follow) for the appropriate date.

- Professional journals and magazines should be separated: Those to be kept purely for reference should be placed directly into the "to be filed" bin. For those that you will actually read or at least skim, place them in a reading file (which you keep with you at all times to use during in-between time). If there are only selected articles of interest, remove them and toss the rest of the magazine.

- Only those items that require action by you should find their way to your desk.

  When those items reach your desk, immediately complete any item that will require two minutes or less. Just do it and get it gone. Other items to be acted upon should be added to the appropriate lists (master, action, next step, etc.) then filed in a daily organizer or a tickler file. If it requires action today, place it in your daily organizer separated into A-B-C priority status. Many people use an expandable folder. If the item requires action anytime other than today, mark in the upper right-hand corner the date it will be acted upon and file it directly into your tickler file.

The Tickler File: Setting It Up and Making It Work

The tickler file is an organizational tool used to simplify the tracking of and managing of work flow. A well-run tickler file enables you to make paper disappear from your desk, only to reappear at the exact time you need it. In the meantime, it doesn't clutter your desk or your mind.

The tickler file consists of 31 daily files marked 1 through 31 and 12 monthly files labeled with the months of the year.

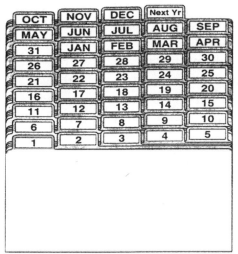

The daily files are in the front, beginning with tomorrow's date. If today is August 6, the front file would be "7." The succeeding daily files represent the remaining days of that month (8 - 31). Behind the "31" file would be the monthly file for the following month (September), and behind it are the daily files 1 - 6. Behind that are the remaining monthly files (October — August).

In short, the upcoming 31 days are in the front of the file with the files for the next 12 months in the back.

Using a tickler file is simple. Let's use the August 6 date as our example. You take your in-box to your desk and you have numerous papers to file for future action. The agenda you've just received for the August 15 meeting would be filed in "15." The one for the September 22 meeting would be filed in September with a 22 noted in the upper right-hand corner. (Don't put it in "22" because right now it means August 22.) When you review a request for a detailed report due to the boss on October 1, you figure it will take you about a week to put it together. Give yourself a little cushion and file that paper for September 20 by placing the number 20 in the upper right-hand corner and placing the paper in "September."

During your 15-minutes of planning at the end of the day, pull out the next day's tickler file (it should be in the front) and assess the work to be done tomorrow. Place the now empty daily file behind the rest of the dailies. When the first of a new month arrives, take out that month's folder (which will now be in the front) and distribute all the collected items into the daily files based on the dates you noted in the upper right-hand corner. Because you made those notations when the items arrived, you do not have to take the time to reread each piece of paper. In short order you're ready to go.

Tip: At the beginning of each month, paperclip the daily files for weekend days and any other days you will not be in the office. That way, nothing can fall between the cracks.

Your General Filing System

There are many options for establishing filing systems. You can file by subject, project, alphabetical, chronological, numeric or geographic. Which you choose depends on how you work and how you will be able to most quickly find and retrieve your documents. In most instances, that is a master alphabetical file with various projects or subcategories color coded for identification.

Time management and efficiency expert David Allen swears that printing file labels with a labeler seriously upgrades the usability of any filing system. Even he admits he doesn't know why it makes a difference, but he insists that it does.

Filing System Tips

- Purge your files once a year. Anything that has been used in the last year should stay in your active files. Anything else should move to inactive. Keep the active files closest to you for quick access.

- Keep your file drawers less than full. If they are full to overflowing, you'll resist trying to file anything else and your desk will once again become a holding station.

- Keep a large stack of third-cut file folders instantly handy. Avoid having papers hanging around waiting for the creation of a new file. Create it and get on with it.

- Name files for easy retrieval; i.e., "Prospects, New" is more easily and logically located than is "New Prospects."

- Use a simple cross-referencing system to avoid making duplicate copies.

- If you travel, use five color-coded, plastic traveling files:

  Traveling In-Basket — catchall file

  Return to Office — completed items to be disbursed or filed upon return to office

  Read/Review — to take advantage of in-between time

  Action Support — information needed for meetings, work to be done, etc., while away from the office

  Data Entry — receipts, business cards, etc. Anything to be recorded for computer or paper reference

- Before you file anything, always consider the probability you will ever need it again. Not the possibility … the probability. Then ask, "What is the worst thing that can happen if I throw it away and then need it?" If the worst that can happen is something you can live with, throw it away.

When in doubt, throw it out.

Never file these four things:

- **Routine Memos:** They are just that — routine. Read the memo, act on it, remember it, and toss it out.

- **Meeting Announcements:** When you get one, immediately put the date and location in your calendar, and toss the announcement out.

- **Directives Since Revised:** Did you ever get a policy memo, then a week later get the revised policy memo? Toss the first one out!

- **Company Information on File Somewhere Else:** Unless you're the person designated to maintain the file!

The classic story on the virtue of tossing out unnecessary paperwork relates that a man who worked for an engineering firm with many foreign clients had just returned from three months overseas working on a project. As you can imagine, he returned to quite a bit of mail and paperwork that had accumulated in his absence.

His first day back in the office was devoted to conferences and briefings. As he prepared to leave work that day, he determined that going through this paper was his top priority for the next day, so he placed it all in a pile on his credenza, ready to be tackled first thing in the morning.

Unfortunately, his company had recently hired a new cleaning firm. That night, his unorganized pile was discovered by one of the workers. The man came in to work the next morning to find three months' worth of paper had disappeared, forever!

7

Catastrophe! Or was it? The impact of this mistake was not immediately known, but as time passed, he reported the following events occurred: One check had to be reissued; two people wrote again, wondering why they hadn't received a response to their first letter, enclosing a copy of the original letters just in case. That was the sum total of the problem created by three months of mail disappearing.

Don't just throw away everything that's piled up on your desk, but remember this story before deciding to hang on to things that are better disposed of.

Finally, you must *make a decision not to add to the problem*. Tom Peters, the "Excellence" books author, once commented that the worst memo ever written "should have been a phone call." Are you choosing the wrong communication medium by putting something in writing? Could this situation be handled more quickly and more effectively over the phone or face to face? Do you really need to have written documentation of the content? If you don't ask these questions, lots of paper will stay in your office unnecessarily.

The Paperless Blizzard — E-Mail

One of the biggest challenges these days is how to organize and manage the flood of e-mail messages you receive on a daily basis. E-mail is really no different from an in-basket or an answering machine: It's a collection box for communication to be assessed, processed and organized. And it suffers from the same challenges — too much stuff you don't have the time or desire to handle and organize as it comes in.

If your e-mail volume and processing speed leave you with consistently more than one screen, you may be suffering from e-mail overhead and paralysis. Set aside time every day to methodically go through your e-mail. Turn off your automatic notifier and check your e-mail box on a scheduled basis, just like you now do your in-box. Keep in mind that everything does not require an immediate response. Urgent messages have proliferated with the use of electronic messaging. But, as organization guru Jeffrey Mayer says, "If everything is urgent, then nothing is urgent."

Handling E-Mail Effectively

- **Don't let e-mail linger in your mailbox.** Once you've read it, file or delete it. Don't waste time reviewing it again later.

- **Create a sufficient archive folder library within your system.** Drag e-mails you want to save only for future reference into those folders. Purge the files at least once annually.

- **Follow the Two-Minute Rule.** Handle immediately any message that can be acted upon and dispatched in two minutes or less. The more e-mail you receive, the more powerful this habit becomes.

- **Use action folders.** For items requiring more than two minutes of focused attention, create folders that are visually distinct from the reference-only folders. For example, if your e-mail program lists your folders alphabetically, you might create:

  @**Action** and @ **Waiting For** and @**Read/Review**

  The @ will put them at the top of the list of folders for easy viewing. Record the action of responding to that e-mail in your organization system so it won't fall between the cracks. If you delegate work via e-mail, make copies to store in your @Waiting folder. The @Read/Review is for FYIs or those that will require more than two minutes to read. You might choose to print these to take to meetings, etc., to read during in-between time.

- **Beware of the Forward feature.** Remember that any e-mail you send can be forwarded to anyone, anywhere, anytime. Always assume your e-mail will end up on your boss's desk.

- **Proofread.** Use your spell-checker. Use upper- and lower-case letters. All upper-cased letters read like you're shouting.

- **Avoid mass mailings.** Don't cc everyone on the planet.

- **No expletives, no personal notes, no electronic chain letters.**

- **Skip the routine thank-you notes.** They just add to the volume.

- **If you want to send an attached file**, be sure the recipient is set up to receive it.

- **When replying ...**

  — Keep original subject headings even if yours are funnier. It facilitates discussion threading.

  — Omit the original text. It adds unnecessarily to the message's length. If the sender can't remember what the original message said, how important could it be?

  — Don't just click the Reply button. Some systems copy everyone on the recipient list. Check your settings.

- **Don't look at your e-mail while you're doing something else.** Check your e-mail in-box when you can give it your full attention so you won't have to reread the messages.

- **Make high-priority e-mail stand out.** Use the colored priority-check option or add colored fonts. Don't overdo this one.

- **Don't write in anger.** Write a draft off-line and wait 24 hours before rereading it. If you get flamed, pick up the phone to respond. You'll be less likely to get into a documented argument you will both regret later.

- **Never send a message you wouldn't want to receive yourself.**

Procrastination

How much productivity do you lose every year because you suffer from the universal energy killer, procrastination? This habit alone costs businesses many dollars and closes the door on countless opportunities.

Procrastination can be defined as delaying anything you need or want to do until later, when there is no valid reason for the delay.

There are a lot of psychological implications that may lie at the root of procrastination. Those who study human behavior generally agree on three underlying causes:

1. **Fear of failure.** This is often expressed as the fear of failing to meet your own, possibly unrealistic, high standards. By putting things off until the last minute, your best efforts, which might not "measure up," are never really tested. What's actually tested is your skill at throwing something together at the last minute. Thus, procrastination avoids a test of your true ability.

2. **Fear of success.** Success has its rewards, but it also has its dangers, e.g., leaving friends or family or business associates behind on the fast track to success. Many people fail at tasks they superficially set out to accomplish while they succeed at maintaining an unconscious status quo in their lives.

7

3. **Fear of surrendering control.** Procrastinators often think that every deadline missed is a battle won in the war to maintain absolute control over their own lives. Constantly arriving late or having your late contribution hold up a project's completion are subtle ways of saying, "I'm really the one in control here."

Other reasons some people procrastinate:

- They imagine they'll have more time later, such as putting things back where they belong.

- They imagine something is not really important, when in reality it is.

- They imagine having no deadlines. "Now that I'm an adult, I can do as I please."

It is important that you do not confuse procrastination with planned delayed action; there are often legitimate reasons to postpone action. Procrastination is the unnecessary delaying of a task that should be done now. Waiting makes sense when you must have more information before you can take action or when conditions are simply not right. The Murphy's law that states: "Left to themselves, things tend to go from bad to worse" is not always true. Sometimes things get better, instead; hence a delay may be a very positive step!

If procrastination is a problem for you, and you're committed to improving your productivity, you can't afford to put off working on eliminating the habit of procrastination any longer. Remember, as an ingrained habit, it can be pretty persistent, but it can be overcome.

Cleaning up the Backlog of Unfinished Projects

1. **Make a list of everything you've been procrastinating about.**

2. **Rate each item in terms of the amount of pressure you feel having it hang over your head.** Note: This is not necessarily the same as importance. Something very important may not be bothering you at all while something relatively insignificant is making you nuts. Rate them on the latter.

3. **Start with the item that is bothering you the most.** Who cares if it is not the most important? Right now you're not doing any of them ... so any step forward is an improvement. Once you've tackled that pressure cooker, you'll feel like the weight of the world has been lifted from your shoulders.

4. **Continue down the list until all are completed.** Be sure to reward yourself along the way.

Conquering Procrastination at Last!

1. **Check your attitude.** Are you a perfectionist? Are your standards so high you are paralyzing yourself? Would an adjustment here make it easier to get things done?

2. **Always ask, "What's the best use of my time right now?"** To clarify this question, in its context here, ask, "If I wasn't doing this right now, would I do it at all?" or "Is it directly related to my goals?" This will help you make an immediate appointment with yourself to get organized and get on with prioritizing.

3. **Get right in front of your answer.** Once you've identified just what to do, get it out of the file and put it on your desk, right in front of you. If the task

requires you to be somewhere else in your office, or even off the premises, go to where the task is. Physically put yourself in front of the job.

4. **Break it down into small pieces.** Too difficult? Too unpleasant? Chop big jobs into more manageable chunks. Taken individually, maybe the steps are not as difficult. Maybe a specific step isn't all that unpleasant. Unpleasant tasks are like the dinner dishes: Ignoring them doesn't make them disappear and usually makes them even tougher to clean later.

5. **Keep a next steps list.** This list is a running account of what the next step is in each of your projects. Just having the next step identified makes it that much easier to do.

6. **Go public!** Make a commitment to others. Tell other people whose opinions you value what you're going to do. Tell them when you're going to start it, and ask them to check on you at that time. A little peer pressure can go a long way, as long as there is something in it for you if you win. This gives you both an incentive for reaching your goal and a penalty for falling short.

7. **Set a short time requirement.** Tell yourself: "I'm going to work on this for only five minutes, and then I'm going to stop." It's not all that difficult to put up with anything for five minutes, and that's all you're committing yourself to. Just five minutes, and then allow yourself to stop. Go ahead and stop after five minutes, too, if you still feel you can't continue your work on the project.

Frequently this kind of experience is like jumping into a swimming pool. To start with, the water's pretty cold, but once you get used to it, it's usually not that bad. If you can do five minutes, you can do fifteen. As long as you're at it, why not keep going?

But remember, you're allowed to quit after the five minutes are up. The worst thing that will happen is you've now completed five minutes of work on this project that wasn't done before.

8. **Stop thinking about it and just do it.** The dread and anticipation of a difficult task are usually worse than the task itself. Bite the bullet. Plunge in.

Avoiding the Pit of Indecision

Many an opportunity has been wasted; many wonderful events have never occurred; jobs and careers have gone down the tubes; precious time has been lost, never to be recaptured. All because a decision was not made. Not a wrong decision; just no decision at all.

When faced with having to make a decision, decide whether or not a task is worth doing and act on it. If it is not worth doing, forget it. Don't let it clutter your life. Simple mathematics can help you determine whether or not a task is worth doing.

Let's say you have a task that will probably take an hour to complete. You put it off for two weeks and worry five to 10 minutes each day about doing it. Total up the time worrying, add a little extra time because you let it pile up, plus the original time required, and you succeed in turning a one-hour job into a 3-1/2-hour project. And that doesn't even consider the emotional drain that saps energy you need to do your other priorities.

People have many excuses for putting off decisions:

• They don't want to make a mistake. As long as they don't decide, they believe a mistake isn't possible.

• They don't want to take responsibility. A decision is a big thing, because its success or failure reflects on them.

- They don't think they have enough information. Sometimes this is true. Other times, it's simply the reason they come up with for failure to act.

- They are looking for the perfect solution. Of course, that means they can never decide, because a perfect solution does not exist.

If you want to be the kind of person who gets things done, you must be decisive and have the courage to act! Don't be deceived into thinking that you can put off a decision indefinitely. You have decided not to decide. Unfortunately, the consequences of this decision are usually far worse than making the wrong decision. And often, the lack of decision-making actually forces the consequences themselves. So the scenario below develops.

- "I should really start on that analysis but maybe I'll wait. The report isn't due until the end of the month."

- The next week, the same choice is made.

- The third week, there is no choice. The report is due Wednesday and a priority crisis erupts Monday afternoon.

In the final analysis, the circumstances forced the decision. The lack of time now presents an excellent reason for turning in a less-than-perfect product, and the person takes no responsibility for not measuring up or failing.

This behavior is even more damaging because it becomes a learned trait that follows people all through life. You can keep indecision from knocking you out of the game by analyzing three questions:

1. **What's the real problem?** What's going on, and why? What is keeping you from making this decision? What, in fact, is the decision? Indecision and procrastination often are close companions at this point.

   If you have a hiring choice to make from among five equally qualified candidates, why have you not decided? Is it too hard to identify the best one from the group? Is there an intuitive, gut-level feeling telling you something different from what the facts may be? Do you not want the responsibility of having chosen one of the candidates? Do you actually feel none of them would work well with you? Is this a position you don't even believe needs to be filled? Are you looking for the non-existent perfect candidate?

Identifying the real problem also focuses your thoughts on the real decision, which may not always be the one you think it is. But you have to see it clearly, or you can't go any farther.

2. **What are the options?** Rarely is a decision a matter of either/or. Life is not black and white, but is filled with subtle shades of gray. You probably have many possible choices you could make. List them on a sheet of paper. If you want to devote space to listing the advantages and disadvantages of each choice, do so. Once this information is in front of you, consider the third question.

3. **Which is a BETTER choice?** Note: the word is better, not best. The biggest mistake you can make is to believe there is one option that is clearly the best of many because work and life are ambiguous most of the time. There simply isn't a best choice, and even if there were, it would be impossible to know which one it is at this point.

If you have several choices, a number of them are probably pretty good. Making a decision is simply picking one of those and going with it.

If you were about to enter a large city, it wouldn't make much sense to call the police chief and say that you weren't going to start through town until someone could assure you every traffic light would be green. Yet many people approach decision-making just that way: If I can't be assured my decision is completely right, I'm not going to make it.

You simply can't see all the way to the end of the road, so go ahead and make a decision based on what you can already see. And, as you travel up the road, continue to do what it takes to make your decision the right one.

Case Study: M*A*S*H

Who can forget the longest-running situation comedy in television history? For 11 years, M*A*S*H sat at or near the top of the Nielsen ratings. Actors Alan Alda, Gary Burghoff and Loretta Swit became household names.

The show was based during the Korean War in a medical unit just behind the conflict. In the unit were highly skilled doctors and nurses, most of whom had been drafted out of their successful careers into service overseas.

For hours at a time, they had practically nothing to do. Then it all happened at once: The helicopters would start to fly in, bringing the wounded from the battlefront for emergency assistance.

Suddenly the quiet hours were only a memory. Each member of the team moved around quickly, in controlled chaos, attending to the critical responsibility each had been assigned. Now, there were too few facilities. There was too little time to do the work that had to be done; too few specialists to attend to the needs; and too many wounded people, all at once.

In those situations, decisiveness was an essential key to survival and success. Somebody had to make life-and-death decisions. The most important decision involved categorizing the wounded into three categories:

- Those who would probably die, no matter how much was done for them.

- Those who would probably survive, even if nothing were done right away.

- Those in between the two extremes. The ones for whom immediate attention would have the greatest impact on their chances for survival. These are the ones the M*A*S*H unit worked on.

7

Unless you're literally out on the battlefront, the decisions you have to make are probably not nearly as gut-wrenching. But, there's a very important lesson to learn from the M*A*S*H unit.

Look at your priorities. Do you have too many? Is there too little time and resources? It's time to decide:

- Are there some projects you are putting lots of effort and energy into that are probably going to die eventually, no matter what you do? Pull the plug. Let these activities die. Put no more time and commitment here.

- Are there some activities that will undoubtedly survive very nicely even if you never did another thing personally? Let go of these, too. Set them free. You'll never regret it!

- What's left? Just like in the Mobile Army Surgical, the priorities and projects remaining are the ones where you have the greatest impact on their success. These are the ones that make a difference — your priorities. List them, arrange them and plan them. And then accomplish them, knowing you've chosen correctly!

There's one more lesson here. Richard Hooker, author of the novel on which the movie and television series M*A*S*H were based, worked for seven years on the book, but it was rejected by 21 publishers. The 22nd publisher,

Morrow, decided to take a chance on it. Only then could it become a best-seller, a blockbuster movie and a highly successful 11-year television series.

Making It Work

CONCERN	REASON	STRATEGY
too much paper	right! there is too much!	develop a paper-controlling mindset
paper backs up on desk	no place for it to go	develop a controlled flow of paper across your desk
too much paper in files	try to save everything	ask question about probability, not possibility
creating more paper than necessary	put everything in writing by habit	ask "Is this necessary?"
small paper projects frequently overlooked	misplaced or lost on desk	start a Tickler File
not enough time to read everything you get	probably is too much	scan things quickly and decide promptly
can't keep up with business or the field	too much information available	choose carefully, then read selectively
frequent procrastination	fear of failure, success or surrendering control	understand your reason and acknowledge it
frequent procrastination	love the adrenaline rush	go on to the next section!
frequent procrastination	poorly developed work habits	apply as many of the seven steps as necessary
worry about upcoming task	reluctance to act/decide	calculate worry time, add to length of job, just do it
delay in decision-making	real problem unidentified	determine real problem, then act
delay in decision-making	want perfect solution	list options, pick one of the better ones—can't be perfect
can't see all obstacles	can rarely see all the way	make a decision, and then make it be the right one

Summary of Key Points

- Move your in-box outside your door.

- Only take action items to your desk.

- Place each item immediately into a daily organizer or a tickler file.

- Immediately complete any action item requiring two minutes or less.

- Be thoughtful and deliberate before you file anything. When in doubt throw it out.

- Review e-mail on a scheduled, not constant, basis.

- Set up @Action, @Waiting and @Read/Review follow up files in your e-mail system.

- Don't let e-mail linger in your in-box. Take action, file it, forward it or place in your @Action file immediately.

- Don't try to look at your e-mail while doing something else.

- Print long e-mails and place in your Read/Review paper file for in-between times.

- When replying to e-mail, keep original subject headings and omit original text.

- Skip routine thank you notes.

- Never send an e-mail message you wouldn't want to receive yourself.

- Procrastination sometimes occurs because the task is either difficult or unpleasant, or both.

- Break large tasks into smaller steps to overcome putting them off.

- Just beginning a task puts you halfway to completion!

- If you have to do something, just do it and don't dwell on it.

7

- Good managers have a bias for action!

- Remember, not to decide is to decide. Have the courage to act.

- Identify the real problem if your decision seems unclear or uncertain.

- Make your decision based on what information you have, and continue to make the right decision as circumstances develop.

- Select a better choice, instead of seeking a best choice.

Putting the Deadly Four to Work in Your Life

1. Have you moved your in-box outside of your line of sight? Specified the time during the day you will check it? Do it now.

2. Set up your daily organizer and your tickler file. Remember to paper clip closed weekend days, vacation days and holidays.

3. Purge your files and separate into active and inactive files. If you can't do it now, select a date, put it on your calendar and commit to it.

4. Purge your e-mail files and set up your archive files appropriately as well as @Action, @Waiting and @Read/Review.

5. Make your master list of unfinished and unstarted projects ranked by the amount of pressure the procrastination is causing you.

6. Complete the most pressure filled item identified on that list.

7. Chart a 30-day course of action. Reassess your progress in 30 days and modify your plan.

> *Action TNT — Today Not Tomorrow*
>
> *No one ever built a reputation based on what they were going to do tomorrow.*

7

7

MY SLIGHT-EDGE IDEAS
ABOUT THE DEADLY FOUR:

CHAPTER 8

Taking Control: Meetings, Interruptions, Telephones

"No one ever has more than 25 percent of their time under control."

Peter Drucker

Meetings: A Waste of Time and Money?

The typical middle manager may spend as much as 25-30 percent of the work day in meetings of one kind or another. Yet, in survey after survey, managers universally point the finger at meetings when asked to name the biggest time waster on the job!

Can we possibly be spending so much time and energy in an activity that produces so little in the way of results and accomplishment? Sadly, the answer is yes. But it doesn't have to be that way.

One of the reasons meetings are inefficient is that most people have never taken the time to figure out just how much meetings cost not only in time, but in money. Calculating time spent isn't really too difficult, but we often forget the multiplication factor. Sure, the meeting only lasts for one hour, but 20 people were involved. In reality, this meeting cost the organization 20 production hours — one hour for each of the 20 participants.

Annual Salary	Each Hour Worth	Each Minute Worth	One Hour/Day For 1 Year Worth
20,000	11.90	.20	2857.
25,000	14.88	.25	3571.
30,000	17.86	.30	4286.
35,000	20.83	.35	5000.
40,000	23.81	.40	5714.

Figure your own: For each $ 1,000 in salary

1,000	.60	.01	143.

240 working days x 7 hours/day
1680 hours/year

The monetary cost is even more staggering, as the chart shows. As you can see, it assumes some very realistic averages: 240 working days per year (there are actually 260 or 261 days, considering holidays, vacation and sick leave) and seven hours per day (eight hours, one for lunch).

A person earning $30,000 per year is paid $17.86 per hour based on those numbers, or about 30 cents per minute. Since most organizations estimate the actual cost of each employee as about 60 percent more than that considering work space, materials, benefits, etc., the true cost is much higher! This employee is paid nearly $18 for the one hour spent in the meeting (more if you count the extras). If 20 people at roughly the same pay level attend, the dollar cost of this meeting is $360.

Now, a question. What if the meeting lasted all day? What if 200 people attended? What if they averaged $60,000 income per year? What if these meetings occurred monthly? Obviously, the potential for wasted time and money is staggering.

The good news is that meetings are not necessarily unproductive any more than dynamite is necessarily destructive. It's all a matter of application. The calculations and monetary analyses provided have been given so you can be effective.

Why Are Meetings So Unproductive?

1. People don't take them seriously. They arrive late, unprepared, doodle throughout the meeting and leave without committing to a plan of action.

2. Most meetings are too long!

3. Digression from the issues at hand is the norm.

4. Little or no follow-up occurs after the meeting.

5. People don't open up and tell the truth. Politics or fear of reprisal minimize forthright contributions.

6. Critical data is unavailable so decisions are postponed, necessitating another meeting.

7. People make the same meeting mistakes over and over again. Their meetings never get better.

Unproductive meetings lead to more bad meetings. Disciplined meetings are about a shared conviction among participants that meetings are real work and should accomplish something.

Chairing an Effective Meeting

1. **Start the meeting on time.** You've called a meeting and invited 15 people. Fourteen of them managed their schedule and time and are ready to begin at the announced starting time.

   Respect the ones who are already there by beginning on time. Only an ineffective leader will make everyone wait for the one latecomer. When the latecomer wanders in, don't even acknowledge the arrival and don't go back and review what you've already covered. You can make the message even more clear if you cover and decide on an issue that person was very interested in at the start of the meeting.

There are some people who intentionally arrive late because they enjoy making grand entrances and the inevitable fuss made over their arrival. If a latecomer frequently disturbs your meeting, and doesn't change his or her ways, you may eventually decide this person doesn't need to be included in the next meeting.

Remember: Making a group of people wait for one late person doesn't just waste time, it wastes money.

2. **End on time.** When you develop the reputation for starting and stopping your meetings in a timely fashion, people will have respect for you and your meeting. They will willingly attend and participate because they know up front just what their commitment to your meeting means.

Did you ever attend a meeting that was to end at 10 a.m. and ran until 11? What if you had made an appointment to meet with someone at 10:30? What if your accomplishments for the entire day were based on having a set amount of discretionary time available, which was now reduced by one hour? Have you noticed the nervous twitches and concerned clock-watching that occurs as a meeting runs overtime? People have places to go and things to do, and permitting a meeting to run over is an infringement on all who attend.

A very effective way of promoting endings to meetings is to use a digital clock in the conference room that runs backward or a timer, like the play clock on a football field or the shot clock in a basketball game. As 60 minutes gradually drops to 20, then 14, then 11, people will pick up their resolve and intensity to discuss and decide.

3. **Have an agenda.** Simple enough, but do you really have one? Specific goals for discussion? A time frame? One with a clear sense of purpose for each item? Are the items clearly indicated as to whether they are for information, for discussion or for making a decision? An Agenda Planning Guide has been provided here to help you devise a complete agenda for every meeting.

8

AGENDA PLANNING GUIDE

AGENDA

Start Time

Topic	Time Required	Person Responsible

Finish Time   **Total Time**

FOLLOW-UP REQUIRED

Topic	Due Date	Person Responsible

4. **State clear objectives and purpose.** What are the major goals of this meeting? What do you hope to accomplish? Why should you or anyone else attend? How will you know if the meeting has been successful? Just like any goal, the more clear and specific, the greater your chances of achievement.

5. **Notify people in advance of the agenda and their responsibilities.** This is helpful not only to the individual person, but to all meeting participants. Tell someone, "You're going to be talking about (subject), and I've allowed eight minutes for your talk, plus five minutes for questions and discussion. Please be sure to include XYZ critical data in your presentation."

   This enables people to prepare for meetings and bring the necessities, such as charts, exhibits, pencil and paper, background information and data.

6. **Cover the most important agenda item first.** This not only pays respect to the people who arrive on time, it also allows people who may have to slip out before the meeting is over to do so without missing as much. Plus, if you've ever attended a one-hour meeting where the first 45 minutes were spent on a relatively trivial item, forcing more important items either to be rushed through or delayed to another meeting, you can see the value of doing #1 first. BONUS: People get in the habit of coming on time.

7. **Make specific assignments.** During a meeting, if a certain job needs to be assigned, make sure it is done at the meeting in such a way that everyone, including the person assigned, knows it. Meetings often end with fuzzy pictures as to who, if anyone, actually took responsibility for carrying out a decision made at the meeting.

8

8. **Control the discussion.** As meeting chair, you can limit the amount of discussion time on any one subject to keep the agenda moving along. If the purpose of an agenda item is to make a decision, bring discussion to a close and make the decision. If it's still at the discussion phase, allow a preset amount of time and control by announcing, "We have time for just one more comment."

   If issues other than agenda items come up, immediately put them into a "parking lot," a list of items to be assigned for follow-up. Before adjourning, assign these items to specific individuals for investigation. Do not allow the meeting to wander off into discussion of these non-agenda issues.

9. **Get input before scheduling a meeting.** If a key participant already has a commitment, or will be away from the office, find this information out before announcing a meeting, so that this person isn't put in a dilemma of having to choose. Also of prime input importance here are participant suggestions of topics to discuss, so you don't have to call another meeting after the meeting.

10. **Invite only those who need to attend.** You've surely sat in a meeting where your presence was requested or required and wondered why you were there when the topics discussed didn't involve you. Keep your guest list to a minimum and rethink it before another meeting in case someone wouldn't need to attend the next time around.

11. **Cut your meeting frequency and cancel unnecessary meetings.** Take inventory of all meetings held regularly. Write down the purpose of each. Is it really necessary? Have some outlived their usefulness? Can any be consolidated? If you're used

to meeting every week, make it every two weeks. If you normally meet monthly, try every other month. Half the meetings equals half the cost, half the time, half the preparation.

If a meeting isn't absolutely required, don't have it. Consider a reasonable alternative. Can a conference call suffice? Can the job be done by an individual? Bad habits abound here, because of habit. Since meetings are an acceptable way to structure work time, you may appear to be productive, but your time may well have been better spent in another activity.

12. **Use computer technology to streamline communication and augment meeting effectiveness.** One simple approach is to use a computer during the meeting to record ideas and focus discussion. Use an oversized monitor for visibility for the whole group. Be sure to generate real-time minutes containing follow-up action items with individual responsibilities specified.

For a more sophisticated approach, explore meetingware and groupware packages (by Ventana, MeetingWare International, Enterprise Solutions and others). These specialized systems use a series of workstations set up in an intranet for the meeting. Workstation participants can respond to questions, propose ideas and vote on options all at the same time. The workstations organize the comments and project them onto a monitor for the entire group to see. Virtually everyone who has studied or participated in computer-enabled meetings agrees that this capacity for simultaneous input produces dramatic gains in the number of ideas and the speed with which they are generated.

8

The Meeting Planning Guide

The Meeting Planning Guide accompanying this page can be used beautifully to plan your meeting, determine its objectives, who needs to attend, what kind of preparation is required and develop an agenda for the meeting.

As you see, it can also be used at the meeting as a way of listing the necessary follow-up required for actions taken and assignments made.

Copy this form and use it any time you are responsible for calling or chairing a meeting. At the same time you fill out this form, do as accurate a calculation as you can concerning the actual cost, in dollars, of the meeting, based on the approximate hourly salary of each participant.

8

Meeting Planning Guide

Date _____

Called by _____

OBJECTIVE
- What should be achieved
  by the end of meeting

MEETING PARTICIPANTS
- Who can contribute
- Who needs information
- Who would provide support
- Who might assist

BACKGROUND INFORMATION
- Information already known
- Further information needed
- Limitations that exist
— date issue must be resolved
— constraints
— resources available

PARTICIPANT PREPARATION
- Background information
  participants need
- How should participants
  prepare before they come?

LOGISTICS
- Date
- Start time
- Finish time
- Location
- Contact person
- Support material needed
  (e.g., handouts, overhead,
  equipment, etc.)

8

If You're Attending a Meeting

- **Only attend those meetings where your participation is essential.** When invited to attend meetings FYI, politely decline.

- **Arrive on time.** Since you have no control over when the meeting will actually start, always take with you work for in-between times.

- **Leave on time.** Establish in advance with the meeting's leader the time you must leave, and leave at the predetermined time, regardless of whether the meeting has officially adjourned.

- **Determine purpose of meeting.** In advance, find out the agenda and know the objectives and purpose of the meeting. This will enable you to determine your purpose for attending and establish respect for your time. Plus, you will be prepared with necessary information or materials needed at the meeting and won't be caught off-guard. You might even ask to have the item(s) most important to you placed first on the agenda Then, if the meeting wanders off course, you can excuse yourself without missing something vital to you.

- **Respect the agenda at the meeting.** You can be sure your important items will be covered because of your advance preparation. Be responsible yourself by directing all comments, questions and discussion to the agenda items only. If there are other things you want to discuss, either set up time for these items to be discussed individually or, if these subjects would be beneficial to all, suggest making them a part of the agenda at the next meeting.

- **Summarize key points and follow-up responsibilities if the meeting chair does not.** This can be done in a low-key way and will help keep the group on target.

8

Rate Your Meetings

Future meetings can be improved simply by evaluating the quality and productivity of your meetings today. Copy this rating sheet and use it repeatedly. Rate each item from 0 to 10.

	0	1	2	3	4	5	6	7	8	9	10
1. Starts on time?											
2. Has adequate written agenda?											
3. Everyone present and prepared?											
4. Follows written agenda in order, without digression or backtracking?											
5. Leader encourages participation?											
6. Plenty of discussion of important points, without repetition?											
7. General agreement by end of meeting?											
8. Everyone clear about outcomes, what each is to do and when it is to be done?											
9. Agenda completed?											
10. Ends on time?											

8

8

Interruptions

Even the most well-planned and well-scheduled day is not immune to interruptions — by far the most universally experienced and frustrating productivity problem. Studies show that people in office settings are interrupted, on the average, every eight minutes. That's more than 50 times a day. If each interruption takes out three minutes, two and a half hours have been lost! Every day!

Striving for a life totally free of interruptions is unrealistic and inappropriate. Just as you frequently require access to other people, so other people need for you to be available. Controlling interruptions is key to increasing personal productivity. Three types of interruptions must be managed:

- Drop-in visitors from outside the company
- Colleagues, co-workers and others from within our organization
- Telephone

Visitors From the Outside

1. **Screen your visitors.** If you have a receptionist, secretary or anyone else who can safeguard your territory, have them run interference for you.

   - "Could I tell _____ who you are, and the purpose of your visit?"

   - "Mr. or Ms._____ is tied up right now. Could I make an appointment for you for a later time?"

   If you are the safeguard of your own territory, control the conversation immediately by directing it with questions such as: "What can I help you with today?"

2. **Meet the visitor outside your office.** If the visit is convenient and appropriate, meet the person somewhere else in the building. Setting up a neutral site for the meeting enables you to have more control over the length of the conversation. It's frequently easier to end a meeting in a conference room than it is to remove a tenacious visitor from your office.

3. **Stand up as the visitor enters your office.** It's a gracious gesture and it gives you control of the situation. If you choose not to talk then, you can escort the visitor to the door and arrange another time to speak.

4. **Confer while standing up.** Many exchanges can be kept brief and to the point if both parties remain on their feet. If you offer someone a chair, and are seated yourself, this encounter can go on indefinitely.

5. **Set a time limit for the visit.** Assuming you are agreeable to receiving your drop-in visitor, begin with a very specific time limit. Say something like, "I have only five minutes to talk right now," and look at your watch as you say it. "Is that enough time, or should we schedule another time?" Note a specific number of minutes, and avoid saying you have a few or a couple of minutes. After setting a time limit, glance at your watch from time to time. It shows your visitor you are serious about the limit.

6. **Develop rescue signals.** This works best with an informed and aware colleague whom you would help in the same way when necessary. At a predetermined time this person enters the room to remind you of something the two of you need to work on right away. Or perhaps a secretary or receptionist could call you after a certain time has passed. These methods create opportunities for you to politely excuse yourself to get back to business.

8

A pocket pager is a way by which you can rescue yourself! Many units today can be tested to make the same sound an actual paging would make. If you can subtly push the right button, you have your own built-in rescue signal.

The Internal Drop-In

Some of the same ideas will work for interruptions from your co-workers; but for these individuals there are several other time-limiting methods available, as well.

1. **Meet with your associates regularly.** A well-planned, regular meeting can eliminate the necessity of some people interrupting you during the day. If a person knows a certain subject will be discussed in tomorrow's meeting, or that a specific time will be allotted for pertinent questions, he or she may not feel it necessary to interrupt you today. (See Chapter 9 for details of the Eight-Minute Meeting.)

   The key word in this solution is meet. If you decide to schedule regular meetings, have them. Make them worthwhile. Respect the time within the meeting and others will respect your time outside the meeting.

2. **Agree on an office "quiet time."** Perhaps you can't control interruptions completely all day, but you can set up an hour each day when you don't allow any interruptions. Appointments should not be scheduled during this hour, nor should people answer the phone. This is an hour in which each individual can work productively, without interruption.

   An office "quiet hour" makes the rest of the day something to shout about! Set one of these hours up at your place of business each day. It really works! Note: You'll find this hour even more effective if you don't use it to plan! In fact, an early hour in the

8

day can actually be the one in which you tackle and complete that top-priority project you determined the night before.

3. **Establish available hours.** Establish certain times during the day when you are or are not available to your people. Not only can you now plan for certain times of your day with no disturbances, you may be doing your people a favor, too. You'd be amazed how many people say their biggest interruption is their manager.

    There's a real serendipity to establishing reception hours. How many times do your people come to you with trivial questions you really wish they'd answer for themselves? If you're not available all the time, folks may solve some of their own problems, or the problem may go away completely. At least they will build up so you can deal with several at one time.

4. **Block interruptions.** Sometimes the physical aspects of the workplace can create problems. Are your desk and its environs inviting to others? Are you positioned so you make eye contact with practically everyone who walks by? Do you happen to be located on the way to the office lounge, coffee pot or copy machine?

    Move your desk so that you don't have to look at everyone who passes. Move the coffee pot. If that's not possible, consider investing in a screen that can block much of the distracting movement. Or ask for a different office.

5. **Remove the visitor chair.** All too often, colleagues and co-workers think that visitor chair was intended for them. Unless you must meet with outside visitors at your desk, remove the extra chair(s) from your office. If that is not possible, at least move it some distance from your desk. You can always invite the right people to move it up closer for better communication. And be sure to place some personal things on that chair such as your overcoat, packages, or purse. While many will remove files from a chair, few people will be so brazen as to clear away personal items so they can sit down.

6. **Close your door.** While nothing is as inviting as an office with an open door, closing that door sends a strong signal to others: Leave me alone. If periods of concentration are required such as when you're writing, take advantage of the closed door and its message. To still maintain the open-door feeling, consider putting a sign on the closed door reading: "Let's talk later. Thanks!" Part of the attitude could be conveyed with a clipboard on which to write messages or questions, or listing the name of who to contact if you're not available.

If you have no door, find another way to signal whether you are available or not. Employees of Hallmark Cards have solved this problem in a novel way. A little flag on each person's desk is a visual availability indicator. When the flag is pulled down to half-mast, it's the signal that means not available.

One creative thinker who works in a bullpen area bought an electronic sign for his desk that flashes BUSY! BUSY! BUSY! When he needs uninterrupted time, he turns it on. Another inventive soul who works in a cubicle hangs a "This door is closed. Please do not disturb" sign on the back of a visitor's chair and places the chair in the opening to his cubicle as a physical barrier to entry.

7. **Find a hideaway.** You can enjoy lots of peaceful, uninterrupted time if you can't be found. When demands press you from all sides, where else can you go to work on them? Is there a conference room that is usually vacant? Another department with an empty desk, where people wouldn't think to look for you? Do you even have to be in the building at all times?

Two executives of a large company had large and luxurious private offices built for themselves. At the same time, they rented an 8-by-10-foot cubbyhole of an office in an executive suites building two blocks away. When they had work that really had to be done, they would invariably escape to their hideaway. Nobody ever found them.

In-person interruptions: We all have them, yet there are many methods at our disposal to help deal with them in acceptable ways. You don't have to lie. You don't have to be rude. But you do have to control your time and work, and these techniques can make a big difference.

Regaining Control of the Telephone

"Watson, come here! I want you."

History does not record the first instance of procrastination on the job. Nor do we have any inkling of when someone's desk first became too cluttered to find anything. The first time someone stayed too long in another's office? Who knows?

We can, however, pinpoint with absolute certainty the time and place of the first telephone interruption. After all, when Alexander Graham Bell invented his contraption in

1876, the first call he made caused Mr. Watson, his assistant, to change his plans. We don't know what he was doing at the time it rang, but he probably wasn't already headed out the door to see his boss.

Although the telephone has accomplished far more good than harm to productivity since its invention, you can be certain that no one has had an uninterrupted moment since the telephone took its place on the desks of the world. Even the introduction of voice mail has been a mixed blessing.

Let's take a look at ways to most effectively utilize these powerful tools.

Dealing with the telephone requires a little creativity and assertiveness and a great deal of self-control and determination.

1. **Decide when you will use the telephone.** Consciously choosing certain times to phone and ignoring the impulses at other times give you much more control.

   - Set aside specific times during the day to use the phone for outgoing calls. You can make each call more quickly and effectively by saving up all your calls and making them in rapid succession. You tend to get on a roll, to reduce the amount of uncertainty about what to do next. As a result, you make each call faster and move on to the next one more quickly.

   - Identify and communicate to others when you will be receiving calls as well as specific times you will not be available to take incoming calls (your prime time!). "I'm generally not available between ___ and ___. The best time to call is _____." Do not continue to routinely answer your phone during times you do not want people interrupting you. If you do, people will continue calling you when you have asked them not to. If

8

you stop answering during that time, gradually they will begin to call when they can reach you. Instead, direct your calls to voice mail or ask someone else in your office to pick up for you. (More on voice mail later.)

2. **Group important calls.** Do several calls deal with the same meeting or subject? Make these calls at one time! Get the reference material out just once, put yourself in the frame of mind the subject requires, and go for it!

3. **Plan your calls in writing.** Before making a call, outline the ideas you want to cover. Make a list of questions you want to ask and leave room to write in answers as you get them. Gather the information and references you need. Clear enough working space on your desk. Have a pen or pencil in your hand as you call.

4. **Focus your concentration on the call.** Here's where the real value of a written outline comes forward. Get to the point. Stick to it. When you speak, be as brief and concise as you can be. What if you would later have to write out, word for word, the entire telephone call? Would you be more careful in how, and how often, you said something?

5. **Stand up to talk.** For many people, the opportunity to make a phone call represents a time to take a break and rest. It's easy to see when this is happening: Is a person leaning back in the chair, feet up, arms at side, cup of coffee nearby?

If you have consciously decided to use this as a break, fine. But if you want to stick to business, and get this over with quickly, make the call standing up. The same effect of meeting while standing up takes over here: If you're not all that comfortable, you tend to stick to the purpose of the call.

8

6. **Time limit each call.** Decide before you call about how long the business should take. Set a conservative time limit and stick to it. Measure the call yourself using the timing feature on the phone system, a watch that shows seconds, or something as simple as a three-minute egg timer.

7. **Develop a set of verbal gestures to sign off.** Sometimes it's harder to end a phone call than it is to get into the business part. You need to have several possible phrases ready to begin to close a call. The easiest phrases to use are those that indicate your concern over the other person's time, rather than your own. Try these:

   • "I need to let you get back to work."

   • "I've probably tied up your line long enough, so …"

   • "I know you're busy so I'll let you go."

   Others relate to the simple fact that the conversation is ending: "Before we hang up, I have just one more quick question," or "Before you go …"

8. **Decide before the phone rings if you will answer it.** Pavlov's dogs were never as conditioned in their responses as most people are to the signaling of the telephone. The responses are never turned off, either.

   Important meeting going on in your office? Deep in thought about tomorrow's speech? Planning a major project? Catching a well-deserved five-minute break with a cup of coffee?

   At home: Are you outside working in the yard? Just sat down to dinner? In the bathroom? Spending quality time with children? Just settled in to watch the television program you've wanted to see all week?

   Somehow, once that phone rings, it becomes top priority. Why? Do you even know who's calling, what the call is about, and how important it is? Absolutely not, but we jump through hoops to answer it anyway. It takes great self-control to ignore a ringing phone and to stay focused on the task at hand. The urge to answer it is strong but your perseverance in ignoring it will pay large dividends in improved productivity.

Of course, if one of the most important responsibilities of your job is to answer the telephone, this advice does not apply to your situation. By all means, answer the phone and don't resent the intrusion. This is a very important part of your job, as your organization's customers or clients rely on being able to contact it.

9. **Have calls screened positively.** If you have a secretary or receptionist answering the phone, the more information this person can pull out of the caller, the more effectively you can use the telephone.

Who is calling? From what company? What is the nature of the call? What does the caller really want? Is there someone else who could help the caller? Could the secretary or receptionist provide all the information or answers the caller is seeking?

The more action-oriented questions asked, the more likely it is you'll never have to talk with the caller yourself. The caller gets answers and you aren't interrupted.

10. **Make appointments for callbacks.** This is another function of screening calls effectively. It often doesn't happen because of the misconceptions concerning telephone messages. A name and a telephone number do not a message make. Who called? From what company or organization? What does the caller want? When is a convenient time to return the call? What's another convenient time if your schedule shows a commitment at that first time?

8

Possibly more time is wasted playing telephone tag than in any other single activity at work. This game can be avoided if message-taking is more thorough and complete.

11. **Return calls at appropriate times.** Yes, this means at the designated callback times, but it also challenges you to think about other ways in which a time may be appropriate or inappropriate.

Fully 75 percent of all business calls go uncompleted on the first try. Be sure to consider lunch hours, time zones, and other factors affecting the likelihood your call will be completed. Of course, if you have no need to talk to the person directly, calling at an off hour and leaving a concise message on voice mail may be the most expeditious way to communicate. Or send an e-mail. Fifty-five percent of all business is one-way-with no conversation required. Use technology to your advantage in these instances.

12. **Get to the point with a smile.** A business call can be divided into three parts: the greeting, business portion and ending. Obviously, the purpose of the call, and the most value-effective part, is the business portion. You don't want to sacrifice any time here. Nor do you want to risk having the call interrupted before you've completed your business.

But the greeting and the ending cause much wasted time. Small talk, friendly chit-chat, beating around the bush and all sorts of things take place before and after the business part. It's a habit. It's probably related to the fact that we want the caller to be glad he or she called.

Can you hear a smile over the telephone? Absolutely. And this is the very best way to get right in to and out of the valuable part of the call. As soon as you know who's calling, smile and cheerfully say,

8

"Hi! What can I do for you today?" The caller has been greeted warmly and enthusiastically and you've jumped right over the small talk into business.

Once you feel the business purpose of the call has ended, you can get out the same way. Smile! Ask, "Is there anything else we need to discuss?" If the answer is yes, perhaps you've misjudged and there's still value to be gained. No problem! When that topic is finished, smile and ask the same question again. Once the answer is no, that's the time to smile again and say, "Great! It's been nice talking with you today. Good-bye."

By smiling and asking a question at those two critical junctures, you have created a pleasant calling experience and directed all the time and energy of the call to the business purpose for which it was made.

Using Voice Mail to Your Advantage

Voice mail can be an outstanding communication tool or it can be a royal pain. Yes, it's annoying to get a voice mail message when you need to talk to a live, breathing human being, but think how much time you save not being put on hold!

Voice mail is available 24 hours a day, seven days a week, thereby facilitating world-wide communication. No longer do you have to juggle time zones. Voice mail is also more efficient when you simply need to pass along information. The average voice mail message is significantly shorter than the actual conversation would be.

8

Handling Your Own Mailbox

Your outgoing message should be informative, courteous, brief and current. People don't like hearing last Friday's message on Tuesday. Record it enthusiastically in a clear, distinct voice. Be sure to include:

- A specific time when you will be available

- Instructions if the caller needs to be transferred to someone else for immediate assistance

- Information about the length of message the caller may leave if you are limiting the length

- Instructions about how the caller can skip the outgoing message when calling in the future

Check your mailbox frequently and respond quickly. One of the biggest complaints people have about voice mail is that their messages are frequently not answered. If you can respond immediately, do so and delete the messages. If you cannot respond, make a dated log of the messages and erase the messages. Better yet, have someone else make the log for you.

Another major complaint about voice mail is the incredible number of messages you sometimes receive. Try these recommendations:

- Limit the length of time for each message to 60 - 90 seconds.

- Limit the number of calls your mailbox will hold. When the caller gets the full mailbox message, they'll call someone else, taking one thing off your plate.

- Increase the playback speed of your calls.

One final note about your own mailbox. Get a copy of the operating manual from your system administrator and familiarize yourself with all your system's features. Many have a number of excellent time-saving bells and whistles most of their users don't even know about.

Leaving a Voice Mail Message for Someone Else

- Every time you make a call, be prepared to get voice mail. Have your message well thought out. State your most important points first, then lesser points later.

- Smile and speak clearly, slowly and concisely.

- Leave your phone number twice — once at the beginning of the message and again at the end. Leave the number even if the person you are calling has it. It may not be handy when he/she retrieves your message.

- When leaving your name and address, be sure to spell them.

In short, leave the kind of message you wish people would leave for you.

8

Making It Work

CONCERN	REASON	STRATEGY
meeting begins late	some participants not yet in attendance	begin without latecomers
meeting runs too long	ending time not set and stuck with	ending time is as important as starting time
people unprepared for meeting	participants not notified of responsibility	assign in advance
no follow-through	assignments and actions not clearly understood	make specific at meeting and log on meeting planner
angry about human and telephone interruptions	productivity affected	recognize interruptions are sometimes necessary
people just walk into your office	it's possible to do so!	screen visitors; make it difficult to get through
can't get rid of visitor	it's too easy for this person to stay	meet outside office or stand up while receiving visitor
can't get rid of visitor	time not respected	set specific time limit, or have someone "rescue" you
associates require you for information, decisions	your time too unscheduled	meet with them regularly, have scheduled "open" hours
easily distracted at work	heavy traffic near desk	block interruptions by turning desk, moving chair
during important activity, telephone rings	we stop to answer it	decide before phone rings if you will answer it
telephone "tag"	insufficient message taken	get callback information, let someone else handle it
phone conversations run too long	ineffective use of time	smile and ask a question to get to business part of call
unproductive meetings	value of time not known	calculate actual cost of your meeting based on salaries
financial position of your organization	employee time not used as productively as possible	use ideas in manual to boost each person's productivity

8

Summary of Key Points

- Meetings cost money. Use the salary chart to determine the actual invested dollar amount. Using those salary figures, you can identify the value of each hour of your time and decide how effectively the money has been spent.

- Meeting planners who start and stop on time and who have a planned agenda they stick with are respected and their meetings are productive.

- Cover the most important agenda item first in your meeting.

- Control discussion both in time and scope.

- Try to meet half as often.

- Identify meetings that are only habitual and eliminate them.

- As a participant, actively involve yourself in timing, responsibility, and sticking to agenda items.

- People are interrupted more than 50 times per day.

- If a visitor has to get past someone else to get to you, many unwelcome interruptions can be eliminated.

- Shorten the time of the interruption by meeting the visitor outside your office and by standing up while talking.

- Being available doesn't mean you are at everyone's beck and call every minute of the day. Schedule reception hours.

- If you don't want to be interrupted, close your door or go somewhere else. If you have no door, find a creative way to signal when you are not available.

- Determine specific times of day to use the phone and group your calls.

8

- You are not required to answer the phone every time it rings.

- Practice the art of real message taking. Take down available times for callbacks, purpose of call, etc.

- Develop your own set of verbal phrases to sign off a call.

- Use voice mail or e-mail when no conversation is required.

Putting Effective Meetings and Controlled Interruptions to Work in Your Life

1. How many times a day are you interrupted? How much time do these interruptions take? How many eight-hour days per year are you losing?

2. How much is your time worth per hour when you are at work?

3. Consider the last meeting you attended. How much do you think the meeting cost? Were those dollars well spent?

4. Look at the meetings you are scheduled to attend over the next three weeks.

   - Do you have a written agenda for each? If not, get one.

   - Is your presence really necessary? If not, how can you get out of attending?

   - If you must attend, rate the meeting using the scale.

5. Who is your most persistent interrupter? How can you handle this person more effectively?

6. What hours could you schedule in your day to be unavailable?

7. If you don't have an office, what non-verbal sign can you use to establish your work space?

8. What is the best time each day to make your outgoing phone calls? How long, on average, need you set aside?

9. Evaluate your outgoing voice mail message. Make necessary changes to make it more effective.

10. Obtain your voice mail operating manual and study it.

11. Chart a 30-day course of action. Reassess your progress in 30 days and modify your plan.

> ### *Action TNT — Today Not Tomorrow*
> *No one ever built a reputation based on what they were going to do tomorrow.*

8

MY SLIGHT-EDGE IDEAS CONCERNING MEETINGS AND INTERRUPTIONS:

CHAPTER 9

Communicating Priorities

"You can have brilliant ideas, but if you can't get them across, your ideas won't get you anywhere."

Lee Iacocca

Communicating your priorities and asserting the validity of your position are two of the most difficult aspects of priority management to master. The foundation is an iron-clad commitment to and an in-depth understanding of your choices.

The development of a reputation for knowing exactly what you are doing and why, and of effectively planning and prioritizing projects are essential to minimize challenges. In addition to strong self-management habits and priority management techniques discussed throughout this manual, several interpersonal skills are necessary to achieve your goals.

- The ability to communicate clearly, concisely, completely and directly.

- The ability to listen effectively to others.

- The ability to obtain agreement from others regarding your priorities.

The better you are in these areas, the easier life is going to be, the less stress you will have, and the more control you'll have over your entire situation.

Assessment: Communications Skills

Respond to the statements below, indicating (by circling the appropriate number), whether you agree (3); are not sure (2); or disagree (1) with each statement:

	Agree	Unsure	Disagree
1. When listening to someone, I always understand what I hear.	3	2	1
2. I always give lots of verbal feedback when I am listening.	3	2	1
3. People like to talk to me because I listen so well.	3	2	1
4. Others tell me how clearly and concisely I speak.	3	2	1
5. People rarely ask me to clarify something I've said.	3	2	1
6. I have little trouble getting people to do what I've asked.	3	2	1
7. It's easy to be assertive when someone tries to use me.	3	2	1
8. I know my boss's personal mission statement.	3	2	1
9. At this moment, my priorities match my boss's.	3	2	1
10. My boss and I meet regularly to go over priorities.	3	2	1
11. I rarely have a conflict with my boss over what's important.	3	2	1
12. It's easy to get others to commit to my plans and help me.	3	2	1
13. I never put something on my list unless I ask "why me?"	3	2	1

9

Total up your score:

29 or more: You have great communications skills; on to the top!

28 - 18:   You sometimes miscommunicate. Don't worry, we all do.

less than 18:   Can it be the whole world's against you?

Communication Precision

When you're working with other people on projects and tasks, the clarity of your own words makes a difference. It's often difficult to communicate your plan to others because you don't have it clearly defined in your own head. And even when the plan is clear to you, your explanation may not be clear to others.

In every verbal interaction, eight kinds of communication are transpiring simultaneously:

- What you mean to say

- What you actually say

- What the other person hears

- What the other person thought they heard

- What the other person means to say

- What the other person actually says

- What you hear the other person say

- What you think you heard the other person say

When these eight items are not in sync, confusion reigns, efforts are scattered, and tensions rise as the priority project falls behind schedule.

Simply asking, "Do you understand?" does not solve the problem. Most people will answer yes if they have any comprehension of the situation at all. Maybe they

9

understand 60, 70 or even 90 percent. But is that enough? That remaining 10 - 40 percent can cause a tremendous amount of wasted time and effort. Here are some ways to communicate more clearly:

- **Be concise:** Make your point first, then fill in the pertinent details to keep the listener from jumping to the wrong conclusion. Use as few words as possible. Prepare key one-liners to condense your thoughts on major issues and new proposals. Formulate your position and phrase it in one clear sentence.

  Television-commercial writers know they have only 15 or 30 seconds to get their messages across, so they pack that time with clear, concise images to make their statements simple and powerful, using words to create the mind pictures that are "worth a thousand words."

  Writing-effectiveness studies consistently prove the best writing is concise. In fact, if the letter or memo runs more than one page in length, its effectiveness drops drastically. The same is true in speech. Keep to the point — don't wander. Know what you are going to say before you start. The fewer words you use, the better your communication will be.

> ### *SHORTER IS BETTER!*

- **Be simple:** Watch your word choice very closely. Just as there are no writing prizes for wordiness, there is certainly no award for being too complex when you speak: Don't use bigger words than are necessary. Use words the listener knows and understands. Unless you are certain of your listener's expertise on the subject, choose familiar, non-technical terms.

  Think about your listener and the situation. Avoid the use of jargon. How much does your listener know about the project? Remember, that person certainly doesn't have the benefit of the time and thought you've put into planning something you already knew more about to begin with.

  Don't make assumptions about how much the other person knows. Ask specific questions. Then make your explanations one step simpler than the other person's responses would indicate is necessary. Most people think they know more about an issue than they really do.

- **Be direct:** Say what you mean and ask for what you want. Use specific language. Avoid generalities and assumptions. It's important to use the names of things (not stuff), names of people (not he, she, they) and numbers (not some or more) whenever possible. Vague language comes from a lack of assertiveness, an unwillingness to take responsibility for what has been said, or not wanting the listener to get a wrong impression about us. In reality, it leaves great voids in the picture that the listener has to somehow fill in.

9

215

Here are a couple of examples on how to be direct:

GENERAL	DIRECT
We have to get on the ball around here.	Each person working on this project must increase personal production by five percent.
I hate to bother you, but we sort of need to go over some things.	I know you're working on the Smith report. Right now, though, it's important that I give you this information.

Directness is uncommon in many fields. People are expected to "catch on" in some instances; and in others, language is used to obscure the true meaning. William Lutz' classic book, *Doublespeak*, addresses the problem clearly and humorously. Here are a few of the examples Mr. Lutz cites:

- In its 1981 annual report, Sambo's Restaurants boasted that the company had "achieved national prominence and publicity." They sure did; that was the year the company had filed under Chapter 11 of the Federal Bankruptcy Act.

- Standard Oil Company (Ohio)'s report in 1982 contained the following sentence: "The realities of 1982, as well as the ordinary changes that inevitably result in ongoing planning processes, have caused some modifications of refinements — which is probably a more accurate description — dealing with timing and degree that do not constitute any significant deviation from past thinking." Say what?

- On the other hand, Marshall & Illsley, a bank holding company in Milwaukee, included a letter to the stockholders with its annual report that said only: "Your company had a very good year. Some of it was due to luck; some of it was due to good planning and management. We hope you enjoy the numbers and the pictures." What a breath of fresh air!

> ### SAY WHAT YOU MEAN AND ASK FOR WHAT YOU WANT!

Directness of communication requires assertiveness. Effective communication is rare because people are afraid to express themselves assertively.

Assertiveness is not *aggressiveness*, which is often when you end up saying something you regret. Aggressiveness shows no consideration for the other person. An aggressive person walks in and totally takes over a situation, mashing beneath them anything that dares get in its way. It's knowing you're standing on someone else's foot, and not moving!

Assertiveness is also not *passivity*. Passive people never finish their priority lists, because they are always changing the lists or adding to them. But because passive people never speak up, there is the tacit acceptance or approval of the new project, no matter how trivial or unrelated to the mission statement it might be. It's allowing someone to continue to stand on your foot. The passive person simply never speaks up. Instead, the emotion and energy are all kept inside. People who do this long enough end up killing themselves by the stress and pressure they create within.

Assertiveness is the firm middle ground between aggressiveness and passivity. Assertiveness is saying, "I have a problem. This is what's happening. This is what it's doing to me. And this is what needs to be done. This is what

9

I want." "You're standing on my foot. It hurts. Please step back."

With a good priority list, it's possible to do this. With a well-thought daily action plan, you can say: "I understand what you're asking me to do. Where would you fit this in the priority ranking I have here? Are you saying this new project is more important than what I'm already doing? If I take this project on at this time, what responsibility can you relieve me of? What deadline can be pushed back?"

With practice, you can become great at assertiveness, so don't throw in the towel because being assertive feels uncomfortable at first. Assertive thinking and an assertive response will always be better for your own mental well-being. Remember, assertiveness is not aggressiveness. Assertive statements can be made in direct, but nonconfrontational, ways. If you've already taken the time to plan and prioritize, assertiveness is the communication key that makes them happen.

Listening Your Way to Productivity

Some studies estimate that productivity could practically double if only people would listen — really listen — to each other! Good listening habits are simply not taught and, thus, not developed. Most of us have had classes on how to write, read, speak and lead, but few of us have ever truly studied the subject of listening. In fact, what many people consider "listening" is merely programming their ears for their turn to talk as soon as they don't hear anything else coming out of the other person's mouth!

Poor listening is the #1 cause of

- conflict.
- work being done over and over before it's done the way they wanted it in the first place.

9

- children not doing as well at school as they are capable of doing.

- divorce.

Obviously strong listening skills are critical for all areas of life! How good are yours?

Assessment: Listening Skills

	YES	NO
1. When someone else is talking, do you sometimes interrupt?		
2. When someone else is talking, do you sometimes finish sentences for them?		
3. When someone else is talking, are you sometimes thinking about what you're going to say next rather than what they are saying now?		
4. When you meet a new person for the first time, do you think you have learned that person's name only to discover two minutes later you have no clue?		

Use these suggestions to improve your listening:

1. **Focus on what the other person is saying.** Listen to the words and listen between the lines. You'll have time to formulate your responses in a bit, but right now hone in on what you're being told.

2. **Make eye contact with your speaker.** Looking someone else straight in the eye pretty much demands you give the speaker some attention. It makes you aware of who that person is and what he or she may be saying. Even looking at the mouth occasionally increases your awareness of what the person is saying.

9

219

Occasionally, you may find someone will not make eye contact with you. If so, look away at a fixed point for 5-10 seconds. When you return your glance the other person probably will, too.

When listening to someone, be sure not to look all around or up and down, appearing indifferent, exasperated or unsure of yourself. Concentrate instead on a fixed point. This gives the individual back personal space and enables him or her to come to you again. Resist the urge to stare, though; it invades the speaker's space and increases the problem.

3. **Close your mouth and breathe.** Don't interrupt. Don't interject a clever comment. Don't finish sentences for the other person. It's their turn. If a brilliant, pertinent thought flashes into your mind and you're afraid you'll forget it before it's your turn to talk, jot down a key word or two you can refer to when it is your turn.

4. **Maintain good body posture.** Whether you're standing or sitting, you can put yourself into an erect body posture with the head and spine straight, which opens up the listening channels. Keep your head still and straight, arms in toward your body and hands relaxed with open palms. Can you really give attention when you're slouched, leaning or slumped in a chair?

Listening effectiveness is directly related to the alertness that has to be present when you put your body into an attentive posture.

5. **Give lots of verbal feedback.** Even if you are actively listening, what you hear (or interpret) may be different from what the other person is saying. Feedback will tell the speaker you're understanding

9

what is being said, helping to ensure what you're hearing really matches what's being said.

This can be done by repeating some of what you're hearing, even by saying something like, "What I'm hearing you say is (and repeat what you think you heard). Is that it?" or "Let me see if I've got this straight ...," or "Are you saying ...? Right?" At this point, the answer will either be yes, which means your listening was effective, or no, which then enables the speaker to repeat and reinforce just what he or she did mean by the words.

Sometimes repetition of a statement and turning it into a question will lead to clarification. For example:

Person # 1	"I can't pay my bill."
You	"You can't pay your bill?"
Person #1	"I don't have enough money until I get paid next week" or "The bill is higher than it should be."
You	"I see. Let's see what we can work out."

Practice with a friend. Ask your friend to discuss a problem with you. Promise yourself before you begin that you will not ask questions, give advice, preach or moralize. Simply summarize the meaning you are getting from what you hear. Listen for five minutes. Your only goal is to get your friend's perception of the problem.

When the five minutes are up, discuss these questions with your friend: What was it like for you to really listen for five minutes? What problems got in your way? What was it like for the friend to be listened to? Did the friend feel you understood? Did he or she get a different understanding of the problem?

9

Effectively listening demonstrates great respect for the speaker, which is especially important during conflict. But it's not as easy as it sounds.

Do Your Priorities Match Your Boss's?

Planning and setting priorities would be easy if (a) you functioned independently of anyone else, or (b) you had wide-open, regular communication with your superior(s) and (c) you always had complete agreement on what was important and in what order. Unfortunately, these statements apply to very few.

Nothing is more frustrating than having your plans and priorities changed. It's hard enough to adjust to circumstances as they develop and situations change, but mix in a disorganized person, or one who loves the power and control from releasing information a little bit at a time, or someone who makes non-negotiable demands on your time, and you might be tempted to give up. Don't do it! You're too close to success now.

Get all your communications skills out, because this is when you're going to need them. Meeting different demands begins and ends with how effectively you communicate. Get your own priorities planned and in order before making the first move. Know what's important to you. Commit the organization's and your personal mission statements to heart. Have the GANTT and PERT charts with you.

First, you must know the priorities of your superiors. If you work for someone who has clearly and effectively communicated this, go ahead to the next section. If you don't know your boss's priorities, here's one way to find out.

Draft a short note to your boss:

• Communicate the new commitment you've made to organizing and managing your priorities.

- Pass along at least one or two new habits from the many ideas in this manual you've determined to work on.

- List in ranked order your three top priorities for the day or for the week.

- Finish the note with a statement like: "If these are not in line with your priorities, please let me know."

This is assertion that generates feedback. It clarifies thinking, feelings, opinions and understandings. But most important, it creates a path of action. If your boss agrees, you know what to do. If the boss disagrees, you'll be told what is important.

What are the best-case and worst-case scenarios here? The best is that you'll find out that your priorities are exactly in line with your superior's, which is a green light to proceed. The worst-case scenario is that you'll find out your priorities aren't even close. But, you still have opened the communications channels in a very positive and constructive way, so the worst that can happen is that you improve your ability to communicate with your boss.

At the onset, you might consider doing this regularly. Do it weekly or even daily if necessary for a while to get the insight that comes from regular and ongoing awareness of your own needs and those of the other person.

How long it will take to establish a foothold for this type of communication depends on the relationship you have with your boss at the present moment, or the amount of authority your position holds.

You may be thinking, "This would really work great, but you don't know my boss. My boss is the world's largest living bottleneck. He loves the control that can be obtained by waiting and procrastinating on everything. If I were to write a note like the one just described to my boss, I guarantee you, three weeks later it would still be lying on the desk, unanswered."

9

No doubt about it. There are many people like that out there. And that's why a little bit of assertive wording can eliminate the agonizing, directionless waits some people suffer through. If you believe your boss would ignore a priorities-oriented memo, consider wording your last sentence like this: "If I don't hear back from you by (and put a deadline you can live with here), I'll assume we are in agreement and I can move forward accordingly."

That's assertiveness. This is not a threat; it is merely a factual option for the reader.

As you build and develop this effective communication of priorities with your superiors, your contact can become less frequent in many cases, and you can keep the relationship fine-tuned by asking your boss for regularly scheduled eight-minute meetings.

The Eight-Minute Meeting

If you and your boss(es) must work closely as a team, you may decide to establish a regular face-to-face meeting. The frequency of these meetings should allow you to maintain contact often enough to have a clear sense of priorities, control and planning. If your Daily Action List and priorities are going to constantly depend on what your boss is doing, ask for a daily eight-minute meeting.

Why eight minutes? Why not five, or 10? Eight is typically about the time needed to cover what needs to be done in this meeting. The problem with lengths like five minutes or 10 minutes (or the famous question: "Do you have a minute?" — which is never just a minute) is that people tend to think of these time frames in very general terms. A length like eight minutes implies a specific amount of time. It commands respect, and gives you the halo effect of being a well-organized person.

In this meeting, you and your boss can:

- Go over both of your calendars, making sure everything is coordinated.

- Review your accomplishments. It can really show someone else just how much you are accomplishing.

- Consider the priority ranking of your daily action list for the next day.

- Discuss possible upcoming events, a heads-up or early warning signal for planning purposes. If you have bad news, pass it along early. People don't like to be surprised. As soon as you know a deadline is going to be missed, let your boss know. Perhaps a solution can be reached. Maybe some help can be made available to you. Possibly, the deadline isn't as critical as you thought it was.

The success of this meeting will depend on you. Whether it becomes a regular planning activity depends on how effective you make it. The value of regular planning with someone you work so closely with is immeasurable. Remember to clarify your own priorities first. Always.

Dealing With the Interrupting Boss or Bosses

Sometimes people develop habits that are hard to break. Nothing is more irritating than having to work with a person who's never organized enough to allow us to maintain priorities or stick to our daily action list. But that doesn't mean you should give up on prioritizing. In fact, you may notice that the more you practice organizing and managing your own priorities, the less some of these people will bother you with their unscheduled requests and the more fun your work may become.

9

Assertiveness is a powerful shield. The more your priorities are identified and ranked, the stronger the shield will be. So, here you are, hard at work on whatever you have decided is the best use of your time right now, and along comes Mr. or Ms. Unorganized with an urgent request. What do you do?

1. **Ask for priority or impact.** It's amazing how some people will automatically assume whenever a boss asks them to do something that the request is top priority. Is it? Have you asked? When working as a team member, someone else's rank may often establish the priority, but remember these words:

> ## *VERIFY AND CLARIFY*

Ask! Be selective of the wording of your question, however. If you ask "Is this top priority?" this person will undoubtedly say, "Of course it is! Why would I be asking you to do it if it weren't?" People like this are good at transferring the guilt, blame and bad feelings to someone else. So choose a question that is open-ended: "What do you think? Is this a medium priority, or what?" Make sure you ask a question regarding priority or impact in such a way that it allows for an answer other than "Yes, it's important." You'll be amazed at how often the answer will be, "Yeah, medium is about right." Great. Now you can fit it into your daily action list as appropriate. If the answer is "No, it's really urgent," you know it truly is a #1 priority needing immediate attention.

How you ask is just as important, if not even more so, as asking the question in the first place.

When your voice is firm, strong, relaxed and self-confident, you will have more appropriate

9

communication with your boss or anyone else. The voice, as well as facial expression, influences others even more than rational, logical facts. This has been documented by many well-established communications studies such as those noted in Dr. Albert Mehrabian's *Silent Messages*.

Stating your questions with confidence — firm, strong and relaxed, eliminates the tone that tells your listener, "I'm judging or evaluating your request." That only puts the other person on the defensive. With assertiveness, your boss always knows when you're simply asking for clarification.

2. **Ask for deadlines.** The question, "When do you want this?" will inevitably be answered "yesterday" or "right away" or "by 4 p.m. today." Yes, this is a deadline. But what kind of deadline is it? We've all had this experience: Someone comes to us and asks us to do something very important, with a really tight deadline. We clear the desk, go to work, maybe work a little late or skip lunch, and somehow get the job completed by the deadline. Five days later the project is still sitting on that other person's desk, and nothing has been done with it.

Let's face it. People do give phony deadlines. They may do that because they don't trust you. If they need it Friday, they think they'd better tell you Wednesday, because surely you're going to be late.

If you ask the question the right way, and phrase it properly, you may be able to find out what the real deadline is. If we ask, "When is the latest I can get this to you?" It sets up a completely different answer than "When do you want it?" Now the other person may say, "Well, I really need it on Friday, because I'm going to use it in the meeting I have that afternoon." Now we know the real deadline.

9

A favor you can do for yourself and for the other person is to beat the deadline by as much as you can. This person has been honest with you about the time frame. Now, honor that trust by showing you can be dependable. Don't violate it by making this person worry up until the last minute. You'll appreciate the peace of mind, and your boss will, too. But the best news is that the more you deliver on time, the more trusted and accurate the deadlines become.

You will also find out pretty quickly if the boss has been honest with you. Sometimes, because standards are not specified, there may really be two deadlines: Your deadline for getting something to the boss and his or her deadline for getting it to someone else. It could backfire when the boss gets out the red pencil and the project comes back: "Rewrite this ... expand on this ... tighten this up, etc." Now your reward for turning this project in ahead of time is more work.

One key is consequences. Keep track of the possible consequences as you respond to these kinds of requests. In the future, it will give you immediate knowledge of whether an item is important or urgent.

The above steps will work for you whether you have one person interrupting you or several. If you are trying to satisfy many bosses instead of just one, there is one other plan of attack that can help you preserve your priorities and stay out of the stress and conflict that may be created by competing projects from bosses who may not even appreciate each other.

The valuable lesson to be demonstrated by this plan of action is:

> *PEOPLE WILL DO THINGS THAT LEAD TO POSITIVE CONSEQUENCES AND AVOID THINGS THAT LEAD TO NEGATIVE CONSEQUENCES.*

Begin by clarifying the importance and deadlines by asking questions. Let's suppose Boss A has already visited you and given you a high-priority project with a truly tight deadline. You're hard at work and suddenly Boss B arrives on the scene with another high-priority, need-it-now assignment.

1. **Communicate the conflict.** Let the second person know that what you're being asked to do is creating a conflict because of the first person's project. "We've got a problem because I'm already working on something Boss A has just given me with a really tight deadline."

2. **Let the asker make the decision.** "What do you think I should do?" Ask this question and shut up. Boss B has created the conflict. Let him or her make the decision as to what should be done. Many times you'll get the OK to work on Boss A's project first if you ask that question.

   Of course, sometimes the response will be: "I don't care what Boss A told you to do; this is more important!" If so, on to Step 3.

3. **Get the asker to initiate.** If, at this point, you try to decide what's best, it will backfire on you virtually every time. If you surrender and take on Boss B's project, Boss A is guaranteed to walk up just as you're getting started. Don't try to resolve the conflict yourself. These two people have put you in this compromising position; they must resolve it. All too frequently, if you work for more than one boss, you become a pawn in a manipulative chess game among bosses to get the upper hand on each other. Be firm. Be assertive. "I hear what you're saying, and Boss A considers this to be a very important job, too. I'll be happy to do these any way the two of you want it done.

9

You and Boss A need to get together and decide which job I should do first, and which to do next."

Once again, remember the behavior principle here: People will do things that lead to positive consequences, and will avoid things that lead to negative consequences. If you don't encourage them to resolve their problem, it becomes your problem, which makes it possible for them to persist in poor communication. People will continue creating conflict if there is a positive consequence to their action. You can retrain them if you keep sending both players away until they can decide, rather than rewarding them for acting inappropriately.

4. **Offer alternatives.** You can help out, of course, through your own initiative and creativity. Is there a way one job can be accomplished without you? Is there someone else to delegate something to? Could you go back to Boss A, show how much you've done already (since it may be enough for that person to work on for a while) and get permission to handle the other job for a while?

Getting Others to Commit to Your Plan

Although everyone has the same 24-hour day, there is a way to dramatically expand what you accomplish in that time and increase productivity proportionately: using other people's time. In management circles, the process is called delegation. In employee-peer groups, the process is called job descriptions, rules of the game, and team spirit. In family circles, the process is called family cooperation.

Whether through delegation, negotiation or cooperation, when you enlist the help of others, you come out ahead. By enlisting others' help, you gain their commitment as well.

Nine Steps to Commitment

1. **Relate your plan to the overall mission.** Get out the organizational or departmental mission statement and demonstrate the current project's connection to who we are, and what we are doing.

2. **Pinpoint the responsibility.** This step involves performance specification: Have you made it clear what requires action? Do you have a PERT or GANTT chart for this project? This visually focuses attention on just what is needed and how it relates to the overall project.

3. **Select the right person.** Knowledge and skill is usually your starting point — who has the physical or mental resources to accomplish this task? Go back through steps 1 and 2 with the person you've selected, and communicate to that person why he or she is the person for this job.

4. **Communicate clearly.** Review the earlier section of this chapter on being concise, simple and direct. During this step of getting the commitment, you want to both give and get feedback on the project. Ask lots of open-ended questions — the ones that really pull information and understanding into the situation. Questions beginning with words like how, what and why foster good communication between both parties.

5. **Agree on conditions.** Communicate and get agreement on deadlines, progress reports, expectations, how you'll monitor results, where the work is to be done, and to whom it will be submitted.

9

This is the time when negotiating is your best tool. Negotiation is what produces cooperation, especially if you are dealing with a peer and have no authority to delegate. When you can't take no for an answer, it's going to cost you something. That's all right. What can you do in exchange, either now or later?

Negotiation will happen in several ways. Perhaps you can convince one of your superiors, someone with the necessary authority, to involve others in your project by delegating. Maybe there are people you work closely with, closely enough to have developed informal alliances. These mutual relationships are designed to help each other out when possible. Perhaps, someone owes you something. Or perhaps you will now owe them something because you can't take no for an answer.

6. **Clarify the degree of authority and responsibility.** One of your most vital steps is knowing who is responsible for what and how much authority each person involved has. We've all been frustrated by not knowing just how far we could go. We've all wished we had enough authority to effectively carry out our responsibility, but it was never given to us.

Only when you know just what you can do is it possible to do the job. Take the time to make this perfectly clear before work begins on the job. What might that other person want to know? Can I get other people to help? Can I spend any money? Are certain tools or equipment available for my use? What do I need approval to do?

How much authority you grant to another person will depend on how well you already know and trust his or her abilities and responsibility. If you have worked with this individual for years, and know exactly how well he or she knows a certain job, you would probably entrust that person with quite a bit of freedom to make decisions. On the other hand, if this person is relatively new or inexperienced, you may want to be kept posted, and have him or her check with you before making certain moves or taking the next step. Either way, the point is the same. The amount of authority and responsibility must be clarified and understood by all parties at the onset.

7. **Provide support and backup.** This individual is now helping you out on a tough job. What can you do in return? Are there any wrinkles you can iron out of the situation? Any other projects or deadlines that can be delayed? Any of his/her work you could do yourself or assign to a third party? Any interruptions, either human or telephone, you could divert your way?

8. **Check on progress.** The worst thing you can do here is simply walk away and expect to get exactly what you asked for just when you wanted it. After all, if the ultimate responsibility for the success of the task is in your hands, you want and need the control of knowing what's going on at all times. You can mark certain dates on your calendar, or write notes to your tickler file, reminding you to check at various times. Getting feedback at this point is critical.

How you get that feedback is your decision. Some people like to have a formal scheduled meeting so the project is discussed in detail. Others prefer more informal updates, which may be more effective in that they're much less intimidating and usually elicit more honest answers. A series of eight-minute meetings could keep you well informed.

9

9. **Evaluate the completed assignment and give feedback.** You can get anybody to help you at least one time. Whether you ever get help again is determined by how well you can give evaluation and feedback once the job is done. Most people want to know how they did; and they are entitled to an evaluation, especially if you ever want help again.

These nine steps guarantee you'll be able to multiply your own time and efforts because you've gained the commitment of others to your projects. Review the list again, and note the ones most important in achieving the desired results. In most instances, #4, #6 and #9 are the most critical. If you can communicate with power and clarity, provide specific directions regarding authority and responsibility, and give prompt and useful feedback and evaluation, you're nearly there! Practice, practice, practice. When these steps become second nature to you, you will hold a set of priceless keys in your hands!

Five Key Questions

There are five questions related to the job that any person wants answered. The better you can anticipate and answer these questions, the more cooperation you'll get. If you want a team of productive, enthusiastic players, you need to give or get the right answers.

1. **What's my job?** The first thing someone wants to know. What am I here for? What's expected of me? When a person knows the answer to this, the next question is ...

2. **How am I doing?** The need for evaluation and feedback is so strong it's part of the second question. The answer needs to be clear and specific, with useful information.

For example, there once was a boss who did not communicate well. One day, wanting some helpful feedback, an employee asked the boss, "How am I doing?" The boss's response was, "We pay you, don't we?" Obviously, employees want quite a bit more than that!

3. **Does anybody care?** "OK. I know what my job is, and how I'm doing. But what I'd really like to know now is, who cares? How much? How are you telling me? Does it seem sincere? Do I feel like anything more than the social security number on my paycheck, or my employee ID number?"

> ### *THANKS IS A NEGLECTED FORM OF COMPENSATION.*

These are tough questions to answer, and they should tell us we'd better be as open and responsive as we can with thanks, recognition and appreciation for work well done. Because if we don't give it, the next question never comes!

4. **How are we (the group) doing?** This question tells us that employees' individual needs are being met, they feel good about what they're doing, and they feel a part of a team.

5. **How can I help?** I know what my job is. I'm doing well, and someone is telling me that. I feel good about my contribution because I know people appreciate my efforts. I belong to a team, and it's helpful to know what the score is. Therefore, what can I contribute to help us become even more successful?

9

Tool: The Delegation Log

If you do a lot of delegating, negotiating and asking for cooperation, it's a very good idea to keep some sort of log to help you to stay on top of all the assignments and not let anything slip through the cracks. The delegation log will do just that.

This chart may be used in a number of ways, but here's how to use it for logging your communications. List the project and person to whom it was delegated in the first two columns. If you already know a due date, go over to that column and enter the information. Then, determine how many times, and when, you want to check progress between assignment and completion.

As a part of your 15 minutes of planning, review your delegation log. Do you need to check on anyone? How will you do it? You can do it formally (in a meeting) or informally, as part of conversation during the day. When you've received your progress information, cross off the date on the log.

Case Study

Jan Warburton, the supervisor of the data-processing operation at a mid-size educational institution, supervises a staff of four people, and her operation has run successfully for five years.

Several months ago, Jan's department was placed under a different manager. Gloria Sherman, Jan's new manager, worked in a different building and communicated with Jan primarily over the telephone and through electronic mail.

Gloria normally began her work day at 4 a.m. She told Jan it's her best time of the day when she is uninterrupted. By the time Jan arrived at work at 8 a.m., her e-mail system contained as many as 25 separate messages from Gloria, most of them jobs and projects Gloria wanted her to handle. These assignments came with detailed instructions and, in Jan's view, represented busywork activities. Even though Jan had already planned her day, the new assignment load usually disrupted her plans.

In addition, Gloria developed the habit of contacting Jan late in the day, about 3 p.m., with other emergency assignments that she wanted done by the first thing tomorrow. Jan often took this work home with her and, using her home terminal, worked late into the night, sometimes until 1 or 2 a.m., getting the work finished so it was ready in the morning.

Even though Jan finished these assignments on time at great personal sacrifice, Gloria often criticized what Jan had done. If Jan submitted material to her already typed, Gloria always completely retyped it herself. If Jan gave her handwritten information, Gloria criticized her for not typing it.

The other workers in Jan's department were pretty insulated from Gloria's work and critical remarks (thanks to Jan), but on days when Jan was out of the office, they too felt the brunt of Gloria's comments and unreasonable work assignments. Jan worried that some of them would leave for other less stressful jobs.

Jan enjoyed her job but often found herself frustrated by the lack of balance in her life. She was also discouraged by her inability to complete her own work because of the numerous additional last-minute assignments from Gloria. Also, even though she knew she did a good job at her work, Jan began to doubt herself because of the frequent criticism from Gloria.

9

Questions:

1. What is Jan's biggest problem?

2. If you were Jan Warburton, what would you do?

What Actually Happened

Jan decided that, even though Gloria's problems included her inability to stay out of Jan's department and micro-manage things she knew nothing about, the biggest problem was her own lack of assertiveness and communication with Gloria. To overcome her problem, Jan concentrated on doing some things regularly.

- Jan began planning her upcoming day the afternoon before, and before she left work (Gloria was long gone by then), Jan sent an electronic mail message to Gloria, summarizing her plans and top-three priorities for the upcoming day. The message included both personal and departmental priorities.

- When Gloria dropped an urgent project in her lap at 3 p.m., Jan responded, "Gloria, I estimate the job you've just given me will take eight hours to complete, perhaps even longer if I take time to type up all the information. Even if I abandon all my priorities right now and work on this project exclusively, the earliest I could get this to you would be 3 p.m. tomorrow. Before I begin working on this assignment, I need to know if this is more important than the priorities I'm already planning to do; and, if it is, if my anticipated time line is agreeable to you."

- Jan began attaching notes to the material she submitted to Gloria, particularly when the material was handwritten, reminding her that the work was not typed because she knew Gloria wanted the project quickly and usually retyped the material anyway.

- When Jan knew she would be out of the office for a period of time, she notified Gloria well in advance of her absence and asked Gloria to provide any input or assignments to her by a specific time, so that this work could be passed along to her people before she left. Then, before she left, Jan sent a summary of her people's priorities to Gloria's e-mail.

Analysis

Gloria liked to show her power by overloading her people. And, even though she didn't really understand a lot of what went on in Jan's department, she insisted on controlling every detail of the work done. Gloria wasted a lot of her own time creating busywork projects and redoing work already completed, usually to make sure her name was on top.

Jan couldn't control much of Gloria's action. But Jan could protect her own priority list by communicating her plans to Gloria, which she did. Further, Jan had every right to expect reasonable deadlines from Gloria, and to get the work done during normal working hours instead of working half the night at home. By telling Gloria as soon as an urgent project arrived about how long it would take to complete and the earliest she could expect to receive it, Jan could defend herself against unrealistic deadlines.

Only when she had a thorough knowledge of her own plans and priorities could Jan assert herself to Gloria.

When Jan began to do this, she discovered a truth about many demanding people in the workplace: These people will push others just as far as someone will let them. Throwing her own priorities aside and giving up her personal time was not beneficial to Jan; it merely subjected her to more unreasonable requests and expectations from Gloria.

9

Summary of Key Points

- Always have your own priorities in order; become known as a person who is always totally organized and planned.

- To listen better, make eye contact, keep good posture and give verbal feedback to the speaker to ensure you understand.

- Good communication is a two-way street. The more concisely, simply and directly you speak, the more effective you will be.

- Learn to assert yourself by saying what you mean and asking for what you want.

- Ask your boss to find out if your priorities are the same.

- Meet regularly with each of your bosses to communicate priorities and plans and to ensure coordination.

- If you get conflicting requests from multiple bosses, pass the responsibility of resolution back to them, rather than doing it yourself.

- Others will commit themselves to your plan if you answer the questions: Who? What? When? Where? Why? and How?

- Give plenty of feedback to people who help you to guarantee their cooperation on future projects.

- Keep a list of tasks you delegate, with progress report dates, to keep jobs from being overlooked or slipping up on you.

- Asking the question "Why me?" of every item on your daily action list will keep you from doing things you should delegate to others.

Putting Communication Skills to Work in Your Life

1. Rate your listening skills on a scale from 1 (awful) to 10 (perfect). Ask several people at work and at home to rate you also. Do not share your assessment with them in advance. Are you as good a listener as you thought? What specifically will you do to improve your listening skills?

2. Pay attention to your communication with one of your colleagues or co-workers. Are you concise? Could you be more direct? Was your tone passive, assertive or aggressive? What will you do differently in the future?

3. List the three most important things you do on the job in your own opinion. What would your boss list for you? Do your lists match? If not, meet with your boss to clarify.

4. Write out exactly what you will say the next time your bosses each give you a "TOP PRIORITY — URGENT" project for simultaneous completion.

5. Chart a 30-day course of action. Reassess your progress in 30 days and modify your plan.

9

> *Action TNT — Today Not Tomorrow*
>
> *No one ever built a reputation based on what they were going to do tomorrow.*

MY SLIGHT-EDGE IDEAS
ABOUT SKILLFUL COMMUNICATION:

CHAPTER 10

Timelines, Deadlines and Project Tracking

"The hurrieder I go, the behinder I get."

Pennsylvania Dutch Maxim

The ultimate goal of any project is completion.

How do you feel about deadlines? Do they cause a lot of grief in your life? Are they stress producers with little benefit to you? Or do deadlines give you a target to shoot for? Do they tell you where you stand? Do they give you direction? Do they give you the motivation and determination to achieve? Are they helping you plan your project for success?

Even though deadlines have caused some stress in your life, you'd probably agree they are useful. But deadlines aren't enough: Timelines are critical. A timeline is an essential, ongoing schedule of steps that must occur over time as the project moves toward the deadline.

The timelines in your projects provide a motivation for action. They enable you to develop meaningful plans, with mileposts along the way to chart your progress relative to a predetermined completion date. In short, the difference between success and failure in your projects will depend on timelines that work.

An old English proverb states:

> ***THAT WHICH CAN BE DONE ANYTIME
> IS NEVER DONE AT ALL.***

Assessment: Can You Set Workable Timelines?

Directions:

What do you already know about timelines? Indicate your agreement to these statements as follows: (3) I agree; (2) maybe; (1) no!

	Agree	Unsure	Disagree
1. I nearly always complete my projects on time.	3	2	1
2. Others willingly abide by timelines I set for them.	3	2	1
3. I know what makes a timeline work and why it can fail.	3	2	1
4. If a project gets off track, I can always get it going again.	3	2	1
5. I know when to use incentives or compliance to get results.	3	2	1

Add your score:

12 or more:	Old reliable, that's you!
11 - 8:	People hesitate before asking you
7 or less:	You're usually a day late and a dollar short

10

Make It Specific!

For a timeline to be useful, it must be specific as to date and/or time. Totally ineffective phrases that don't work include:

- "Please advise"
- "As soon as possible"
- "At your earliest convenience"
- "When I get around to it"

All of these phrases provide built-in automatic excuses for not performing: It wasn't convenient. I couldn't get around to it.

A specific timeline should not only spur people to action, it should do so in a positive way. It's unhealthy when a timeline pushes you or others against such tight constraints that it's virtually impossible to achieve. Therefore, whether you are establishing your own timelines, working with somebody else's, or setting a timeline for others, you need to recognize the three types of timelines that actually work:

1. **A reasonable timeline.** How much work is required? How much time is available? What else needs to be done at the same time? Is this realistic and reasonable? Add 25 to 50 percent to your original time estimates to make them more realistic. Most people seriously underestimate what will be required for most projects.

    If you or someone else believes the date or time of a timeline is indeed reasonable, there is every reason to expect the timeline will be met. It's a conscious decision, but the subconscious operates strongly in these situations as well. When there's a deep-down-inside feeling of impending failure, achieving the timeline becomes unlikely.

10

Remember, it's always more acceptable to negotiate a reasonable timeline at the beginning of a project than at the end. This helps you establish your planning effectiveness rather than emphasizing your inefficiency.

2. **An equitable timeline.** Is this timeline fair to you if you accept? Are you already overburdened with responsibilities and tight time frames? Are you being penalized for your productivity? Often the reward for people who get the job done is to throw that much more at them!

    If it is not equitable, establish some facts here. A GANTT chart is an excellent tool to visually verify all that is being required from one person or department. This is the time to focus on facts, not personal opinions.

    If people believe they're being dealt with fairly with regard to the work required and the timeline, they can and usually will work within it.

3. **A self-imposed timeline.** No timeline will work for you until you personally commit to it. Of course, many times you set your own timelines, and presumably the time frame you have chosen is also realistic and equitable.

    Do a self-assessment. Are you buying into all three aspects of a timeline at this point? If you are, this will ensure a proactive position toward achievement instead of later assuming and reinforcing a passive victim position, which is never healthy.

    What about the times when someone else sets a timeline for you? The timeline will be achieved if you commit to it and essentially accept it as your own timeline. At that point, it is not somebody else's timeline: It belongs to you. It has become self-imposed. It is yours.

Getting Commitment From Others

How can you get someone else to accept the timeline you set? The same process must take place. The timeline must be reasonable and it must be fair for the other person to decide to take ownership. It is now self-imposed, and should be achieved.

To get the other person to that point, here are a few key questions you can ask to help establish your position:

- "Does this time frame seem realistic to you?"

- "What obstacles do you see that might prevent you from achieving this deadline?"

- "What are some reasonable intermediate goals we could set here?"

- "Is it fair for me to assume you're going to be able to do this?"

- "Can I count on you to have this back to me by (date)?"

A key point to remember here:

> *A PROJECT DOESN'T JUST GET SIX MONTHS BEHIND...IT SLIPS DAY BY DAY, WEEK BY WEEK!*

That's why tracking each project step by step with a flow chart is essential. (A detailed discussion of flow charts appears later in this chapter.)

10

OK, But Something Came up on the Way to Completion

The most realistic, fair, self-imposed timeline can still encounter unexpected difficulties as events develop. Because other priorities arise, suddenly a project that was going so well can be placed on the back burner. A once-realistic timeline is now a huge, negative, demotivating factor. Somehow you're suddenly way off the track, and you're not even sure how you got there.

You have ten options to get a sidetracked project back on course. Choose one that works to get you rolling again.

1. **Renegotiate the timeline.** Perhaps all you need to recover momentum is to get some relief from the timeline. It may be possible for you to go back to the person to whom you committed yourself and get a change or extension, particularly if the circumstances make this reasonable. Perhaps now you will find out if the first timeline you committed to is the real timeline or simply someone else's wish list. With a timeline change, you're no longer behind the program; and you're rolling again.

2. **Re-examine the timelines within the project.** If you're seriously behind schedule, look at your flow charts. Were you able to build a flow chart with a cushion or two in the schedule? Or if you have used up the cushion already, what individual step can be shortened or sped up? Maybe there's a step that involves the mailing of a draft of a report to someone else. This might be a great time to send it by overnight delivery, put it on the fax machine, or e-mail it.

3. **Eliminate the nonessential.** Are some steps in your plan ones you thought would be nice to have, but aren't really critical to the success of your project?

This could be the time to eliminate them. Does it have to be this big? Maybe it's time to downsize a little. Perhaps the final result won't be quite as elaborate, but cutting out a few frills may be just the thing to get your project going again.

This could be a way to provide help for the perfectionist. Some people, when given more than enough time to complete a project, fill all the time by adding nonessential elements, which is actually a form of procrastination. By consciously eliminating nonessential items before you start, you may be able to set a timeline that is tight enough to force the perfectionist to stick to the project. The project never gets off track in the first place.

4. **Expand Your Resources.** What resources do you have? Is it possible to get any more? More people? More equipment? More money? More ideas? What would make a difference here? There's almost always a point in any project when so much time and money has already been invested that spending a little more is worth it. For example, construction companies often get this kind of motivation through the agreement (in the beginning) to substantial daily penalties for each day a project runs past its agreed deadline.

The incentive can also work the other way. The city of Seattle promised a company $18,000 per day for every day it could beat the deadline for completing a storm-damaged bridge over Lake Washington. That's the amount the city calculated it cost each day not to have the bridge operational.

5. **Substitute something else.** Is there a certain item you need for your project that you just can't seem to obtain? Would something else that is already available work as well? Would the substitution make any qualitative difference in the finished project?

10

Many products have come about because of substitution. This could be an asset defined by a liability. The story behind the "Post-It" note paper is a classic illustration. Ask 3-M if it was worth the millions of dollars that have been earned because someone found a substitute use for a glue that didn't stick!

6. **Alternative sources.** Where or how else could you obtain what's holding you up? Is there another source or another way you could do it? A supplier who's been asking for a chance to do business with you? When can your supplier get the materials to you? Is it already in their warehouse? What if you got it yourself instead of waiting for a delivery?

   This philosophy is well explained by Roger Von Oech, author of *A Kick in the Seat of the Pants*, who suggests looking for another right source or solution. If you ever found the best way to do a job, how would you know you had found it? Your second choice could actually end up being better than your first!

7. **Accept partial delivery or shipment.** Suppose your entire mailing is being held up because the 10,000 envelopes aren't available. Call the supplier. Are any of the envelopes printed yet? 2,000 of them? Great! You'll accept a partial delivery now to give you something to start with while your supplier finishes the order.

8. **Incentives.** Here's where the human-relations side of getting your projects back on track enters into play. What kinds of rewards, either for yourself or for others, might spur renewed commitment to the project? The "carrots" of life are sometimes strong enough to do a job nothing else can do.

9. **Compliance.** Likewise, the compliance factors can be effective, too. Sometimes the avoidance of bad consequences is an even stronger force than the pursuit of good consequences.

   In working with people, consider both the incentive and compliance options. April 15 is a good example of this. Think about the lines of people at the post office at midnight turning in their tax returns! Yet, many tax preparers offer the early-return incentive of "get your refund sooner." The same date provides incentive for some people, and compliance for others.

10. **The All Out Question.** If your life depended on it, what could you do to complete the project on time? Identify and evaluate all options; then implement

10

> *IF YOU SET THE RIGHT KIND OF TIMELINES TO BEGIN WITH, THERE ARE MANY WAYS YOU CAN GET YOUR PROJECT BACK ON TRACK!*

suitable ones based on the nature of the consequences of missing your deadline.

With proper tracking, even the most complicated project can be modified before the obstacles/delays become critical time elements. Imagine you're a scientist working with NASA on the Space Shuttle program. You are the person responsible for planning the next launch. You have all of NASA, its suppliers and resources at your disposal. Any person you ask will do exactly what you want him or her to do. You don't actually have to do any work yourself on the project. You're responsible for only one thing: Developing and implementing a plan covering all the steps that must take place before the launch date.

Sound like an easy job? How many factors do you think you'll have to consider? Let's see, there's the weather. The orbits of the satellites your shuttle is going to connect with several thousand miles over the earth. The selection and training of the astronauts. The experiments that will be conducted during the flight. The landing site, the people and equipment that need to be there. The actual rockets that will launch the shuttle spaceward. You'll need to take care of the newspeople who will report on the event and controlling the crowds of spectators. Is the job big enough for you yet?

Of course, these factors only scratch the surface of the literally thousands of steps and thousands of people who'll have to work on the project, in complete coordination, so that everything comes together at one time and the launch is a complete success. If you're ready to turn in your resignation before this job even starts, you'll understand why the world owes the space program a debt of gratitude for the flow charts and tracking processes that were developed to enable just that kind of activity to take place successfully.

Assessment: Flow Charts

Read the statements that follow and circle the number that best describes your response: (3) agree; (2) not sure; (1) disagree:

	Agree	Unsure	Disagree
I currently know the status of all my projects	3	2	1
It's easy to communicate jobs and deadlines to others	3	2	1
If a project falls behind, I know it right away	3	2	1
If a project falls behind, I know why it happened	3	2	1
If I have time problems, I always know well in advance	3	2	1
I regularly use flow charts in planning projects	3	2	1
I usually think backwards when I plan out a project	3	2	1
I build a cushion in my schedules to allow for emergencies	3	2	1

10

Interpretation:

19 or more: Pass the big jobs your way!

18 - 13:   With a little luck, you often get it done, and on time.

less than 13:   People shouldn't put their hopes or money on you!

The Benefits of Flow Charts

The benefits of flow charting to track projects and priorities are numerous.

- **Show the interrelation of activities.** A picture is truly worth thousands of words. As you can see, graphic techniques help others visually understand why a certain step is important and how it relates to other aspects of your project. Without a flow chart, it is often very difficult to explain the necessity of a certain step or timeline.

- **Aid in communicating with others.** The importance and value of dates and delegations is underscored by the flow chart. Once people see how they are part of an entire picture, they're more likely to understand why it's necessary for them to complete their portion of the project within the deadline they've been given.

  One of the best communications benefits of flow charts occurs when you have a peer or superior who comes up with great last-minute ideas like "How about pushing the completion date for this project up by one week?" Don't argue, but don't accept! Immediately get out your flow chart and use it to communicate what needs to be said. If the new deadline is important enough, what other concessions need to be made? What other project needs to be delayed? "I'll be happy to get this done seven days earlier, if you can help me figure out where I can make up the time." This is an opportunity to negotiate with clear and open communication.

Other benefits of using flow charts are:

- **Flow charts help you keep track of large projects with many steps.** It's very difficult for anything to be overlooked when it's a part of a large plan displayed in a flow chart. Perhaps only one person has the complete plan and knows all that is going on and who's doing what, but nothing is lost on the master chart.

- **Flow charts help you turn large steps into small ones for delegation.** Perhaps you can't totally turn a phase of a project over to someone else, but as your flow charts divide the project into specific, individual steps, it is often easier to identify particular activities that can be delegated. Flow charts also demonstrate the value of what's being assigned, helping you delegate more effectively as you can show each individual just how their part relates to the entire project.

- **Flow charts help you reduce time and cost by identifying trouble spots as they occur.** Never again will you suddenly have to divert large groups of people, or great amounts of money, to deal with unexpected crises. Big problems simply don't sneak up on you with a well-planned flow chart. You can effectively manage your time, your people and your money in ways you never thought possible!

- **Flow charts give you immediate knowledge of the impact on your deadline.** If a step takes two days longer to complete than planned, you can look at a flow chart and know instantly if this is a problem and, if so, how much a problem it may be. Did the delay occur on your critical path? Is the delay creating a new critical path? You won't have to guess — you'll know.

Thanks to flow charts, you will never get close to the deadline for a project, discover you're three weeks behind schedule, and not know how it happened. In fact, when a project is finished, review the entire flow chart, analyze what happened and why, and retain this knowledge to make the next flow chart even more accurate and effective!

10

A word of caution: The first few times you develop a flow chart, it may have some weaknesses. If you've never done a certain project before, some of the dates may be guesswork. That's why you can learn so much from flow charts you have finished, and why your ability to plan with accuracy will improve the more you do it.

Project Management/Tracking Software

The bigger and more complex your project, the more useful a computer program can be for you. Computer software that can handle flow charts is abundant and generally very good. Some are industry specific; many are universal. All are constantly being replaced by newer, better models with more bells and whistles.

With a project management tracking program, you can continually update your charts with input as activities are completed and deadlines are met or missed. The revised version is always as clean and neat as the original. Most programs create a "red flag" as deadlines near or problems develop. Some use information from multiple flow charts to point out potential problem areas. For example, if, on three different flow charts, you assigned 84 hours of work to one person in one week, some programs will alert you to this problem.

Determining which software package best suits your needs will require an in-depth evaluation of your project complexities, preferred methods, and the capabilities of the various programs. Some areas to consider include:

- Connectivity with various database platforms
- Number of projects to be tracked
- Number of detail activities per schedule

- Use of multiple schedules and subproject schedules with one project
- Translators for other project management products
- Integrated usage and costs in real-time
- Technical, span and baseline progress modes
- Types of analyses used (CPM, PERT, Resource Loading, etc.)
- Forms of data accepted and displayed (bar charts, histograms, network diagrams, tables, PERT, GANTT, etc.)
- Roll schedules for executive summaries
- Networking capabilities

The list could go on ad infinitum. Check the Internet for the most up-to-date information. A search by "Project Management Software" will generate an abundance of hits or start with any of these producers of project management/tracking programs.

10

ABT Corporation	Projectware	TimeScope
MicroPlanning International	Safari Software Products	Kidasa Software Inc.
Microsoft	Allegro Products Inc.	Artemis
Advanced Management Solutions	SoftLanding Systems	Primavera
Creative Technology Laboratories	IntraPlan	Pictdata Productions

Three Flow Charting Giants: PERT, CPM and GANTT

How The PERT Process Began

The PERT chart owes its beginnings to the Polaris missile program of the mid-1950s. The basic concepts devised by some brilliant minds at that time are now used by people everywhere, in all walks of life. By the end of this chapter, you will be able to use these concepts, too.

When multiple projects have to take place, involving multiple steps and people, you can turn to the information presented here to bring it all under control. Once you learn it, it's not only productive, it's fun!

A Simple PERT Introduction

PERT is an acronym that stands for "Program Evaluation and Review Technique," the lengthy name originally applied by the Polaris scientists to their tracking process.

A PERT chart, even the most simple one, involves four elements:

- **Circles** — in which completed activities are written
- **Lines** — showing the direction of progress and indicating work in progress but not yet completed
- **Dates** — completion targets, i.e., deadlines
- **Names** — of people to whom various responsibilities have been delegated

There's one other element that distinguishes the PERT chart from other methods of planning:

Not only does this process offer new methods of presenting the planning we have done, it forces us into a new thinking pattern as well! In a typical planning process, we ask ourselves "Where am I now?" and then proceed to think in a step-by-step sequence until we eventually reach the end. PERT reverses the process. In PERT, we do our thinking in reverse.

The principle is more logical than it might sound at first. For example, have you ever watched professional golfers on television? Good golfers nearly always think backwards. A professional golfer approaches the tee to play a par-5 hole, that is one in which the target is to play in five strokes or fewer. These are the longest holes on the course, which is why more strokes are required. But, to a pro, the long holes always represent the best chance to go under par, to play the hole in four strokes, known as a "birdie" instead of five.

Before that golfer ever hits the ball, a backwards thought process occurs. "Where is the flag located on the green today?" Then: "Where should my ball land on that green to give me the best chance of a reasonable putt into the hole on my fourth stroke?"

Once that question is answered: "Where does my ball need to end up on the fairway to give me the best approach shot (the third stroke) to that part of the green? Where does my second shot need to be hit from if that's where I want the approach shot to be? What club do I need, and how should I drive the ball off the tee, to put myself in that position?"

Backwards thinking really does work! There are some other advantages, as well:

- Thinking backwards makes you work a little harder and concentrate more.

- Sometimes you can see things going backwards that you miss going the other way.

10

Try Something Easy First

A simple illustration can get you started; a more complicated one will follow.

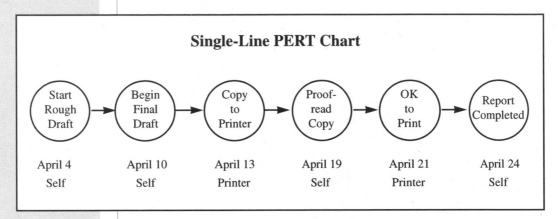

Single-Line PERT Chart

Start Rough Draft	Begin Final Draft	Copy to Printer	Proof-read Copy	OK to Print	Report Completed
April 4	April 10	April 13	April 19	April 21	April 24
Self	Self	Printer	Self	Printer	Self

The first illustration is a single, straight-line chart. It is made up of only one series of steps leading to a completed project, each one taken in order with nothing happening elsewhere. The diagram you see above already has the information filled in. This project is a report, with a deadline date of April 24. The last step, the right-hand circle, is labeled: "Report Completed." The deadline is shown, and we've indicated self as the person responsible for this step.

How did we get all the rest of the information? By working through the project backwards. The question you always want to ask is: "In order for this step to be accomplished, what had to happen just before that?"

This particular report, we decided, is so important we'll secure the best production help available. We're going to have the copy professionally typeset and printed, and thus, the last step before completion reads: "OK to Print," meaning we've given the typesetter permission to proceed with printing the final manuscript. We delegated the printing to the printing company, of course, and the company informed us it needs three days after getting the typeset

10

manuscript to provide us with the finished product. Therefore, the date for giving this "OK to Print" must be no later than April 21, still leaving us three days to get it on the 24th when we need it.

What had to be done before we could give the press an approval to run? Possibly a lot of things, but we've simplified this example down to "Proofread the Copy." We delegated this step to ourselves, once again, and determined it will take two days to complete this step. Therefore, our starting date for this activity must be no later than April 19.

As you can see, the only completion date on the PERT chart is the final date at the right end. All the other dates are start dates. You can infer from this that the completion date for the previous step is the same as the start date for the next step!

We know the dates we're using are going to cross over weekends. To make it easier, we'll assume no weekends and all working days. In creating your own PERT charts, be sure you account for weekend days and holidays. If you're using a tracking software program, it should do that automatically.

Once again, thinking in reverse, what has to happen before we can start proofreading? Well, at some time the copy has to be typeset so we can proofread. Let's call that the previous step, to be done by the printer, who told us to allow six days for this step. This means, as you see, the copy must go to the printer (the start date) no later than April 13.

The copy has to be written. Do you think we ought to have two drafts? We did, which is why the next step to the left reads: "Begin final draft." We allowed three days for finishing the final draft. We must begin, therefore, on April 10.

Finally, before the final draft can begin, there's going to be a rough draft. We've estimated six days to do this. We have to start on April 4 to reach our deadline of April 24 for the finished product.

10

We now have this entire project broken down into a straight line of six steps, each with a starting date and a person responsible assigned to the step. Does this look like it would work? Does it seem reasonable?

Two interesting points here. Suppose we were to put our plans for this report down on paper as we have done, working our way back to the start date and determining we needed to start on April 4, but today is April 6. We have a time problem. But there's very good news. We found out that we had a time problem at the very beginning of the project. Unfortunately, we usually discover a time problem at the very end. When we know about it right away, we have many more options available to us. What could we do today to make up the two lost days in the schedule? Could we delegate out some more work? Could we delay some other project to give us more time on this one? If we got more help, would that make a difference? Could we go to the person who will receive this report and get a two-day extension?

So, even when you have a problem, it's easier to overcome if you've done this kind of planning up front.

Another important thought: Be realistic. Do yourself a favor, in fact, and even try to build a little extra time into your plan. It's frustrating when the first time things don't go as they should and you end up in time difficulties. So add some cushion into your plan.

Before moving on to the next illustration, you might want to complete the PERT Personal Project at the end of the chapter to get familiar with the process.

Time to Move on to a Bigger Project

For our next example, we'll use the production cycle of one of the books published by the NCAA: Official NCAA Ice Hockey Guide. This was a combination of two books, actually: the playing rules and a fan publication containing schedules, records, stories and photographs. Once again, the

10

information is already filled in so you can see the steps we'll describe here. Also, although we worked the planning process through from right to left once again, it is easier to explain going the other direction, so that's the way we'll go.

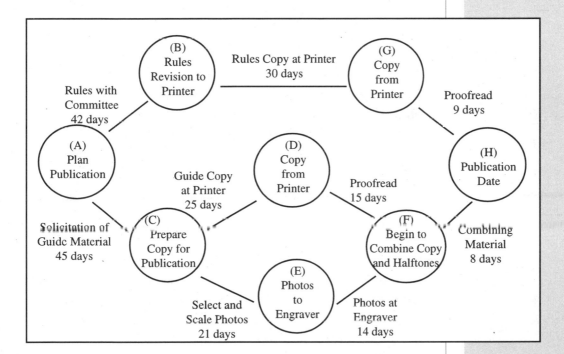

The first project deadline given was the publication date (H on the diagram): The book always had to be out by late September because officials' clinics were held then and the season began by early November.

On the left end is the planning time (A) for the publication. We already know the rules will make up half the book, so our first step was to make up workbooks for the committee to use at its annual rules meeting (this occurs along the line running from A to B, where changes to the rules will be made).

In the meantime, we must send out mailings to solicit all the other material for the Guide part of the book. From each member school we need last year's records, next year's schedule, photos, pre-season prospects, etc. This process is going on along the line from A to C.

Finally we reach a deadline for information, after which we will not be able to use material (C). Once that deadline is reached, we begin to prepare copy to send it to the printer (C to D).

While the printer has the copy, however, there's still a lot to be done. We can begin selecting and scaling the photographs to use in the book (C to E). Once this job is done, we will send the photos to the engraver to make halftones for publication (E to F).

Meanwhile, typeset copy is starting to come back from the printer, so proofreading is begun (D to F). At the junction of these two lines (F), the proofreading is completed, the halftones are on hand, and along the line from F to H we are combining this material to finish the Guide portion.

Don't forget the rules! Once the rules get back from the committee (B), copy will need to be prepared and sent to the printer for revision (B to G). When the revisions are back from the printer (G), there is still a little proofreading to be done on these (G to H).

If everything works out as planned, at letter (H) all the elements of the book come together and are completed, at which point the printer is given the OK to print.

As the previous flow chart displays, even when a lot of different things have to be going on at the same time, each can be tracked with the PERT chart.

The PERT Worksheet

Unless you want your PERT chart to be a big, useless mess of lines and circles, it helps to do some preliminary thinking about just what is happening — what steps might occur and which activities must precede each step in the process.

A linear worksheet is a good way to start, because it allows for lapses in thinking and also provides an easy way to assemble the material in a logical order prior to drawing out the PERT chart.

NOTE: Before beginning the following exercise, copy the PERT Worksheet so you can use it again and again.

10

Project: _____

Start Date: _____

Activity	Preceding Activity	Time Required
___ _____	___ _____	_____
___ _____	___ _____	_____
___ _____	___ _____	_____
___ _____	___ _____	_____
___ _____	___ _____	_____
___ _____	___ _____	_____
___ _____	___ _____	_____
___ _____	___ _____	_____
___ _____	___ _____	_____
___ _____	___ _____	_____
___ _____	___ _____	_____
___ _____	___ _____	_____
___ _____	___ _____	_____
___ _____	___ _____	_____
___ _____	___ _____	_____
___ _____	___ _____	_____

Description: _____

_____

_____

_____

10

Exercise: Developing a PERT Worksheet

Directions:

1. At the top of the sheet, write in the name or description of the project you're planning and put today's date (or your anticipated start date) in the blank.

2. At the bottom of the page, write a detailed description of the completed activity — what it will be, what it will look like, or anything that gives you a clear picture of what form this project will take upon completion. If you know the deadline for the project, place it in the blank provided.

3. Complete the Activity column by starting your list at the bottom of the page, writing in the final activity required before the project is completed. Then, using the backwards-thinking process, work up the page, listing the activities in reverse order. You may not use all the blanks if your project does not require too many steps. Remember the question you'll want to keep asking as you plan backwards: "What prior activity or activities must be completed before this activity can begin?"

    NOTE: No doubt you'll occasionally overlook some steps; the blanks in the chart are wide enough to allow you to insert other ideas that come to mind later.

4. Start at the top of the list and letter the activities alphabetically along the left side, beginning with "A" as the first activity. If you get through the entire alphabet, continue with "AA," "BB," etc.

5. Fill out the "Preceding Activity" column, again starting at the bottom of the list. Use the letter you have assigned to each activity to identify it, rather than writing the activity out again. If your thinking

10

has been fairly clear and complete up to this point, much of this step will be easy. For example, if the last activity is "T," probably the activity just above it on the list ("S") would be listed as the preceding activity, and you'd write "S" in the blank. Sometimes more than one activity must precede a specific step, which will be represented by a branch in the PERT chart, so you may write more than one letter in the preceding activity column.

6. Estimate the time required for each activity, and put the number of hours, days or weeks in the Time column.

7. When you have completed all parts of the PERT Worksheet, you will be able to take this information to draw a PERT Chart, using lines and circles to show all the activities visually.

PERT Worksheet
The Critical Path Method (CPM)

The Critical Path Method was developed separately from PERT, but as it is used today, is usually not actually a separate flow chart. Instead, it becomes a part of a PERT chart. The Critical Path is defined as:

> *THE ACTIVITY LINE THROUGH A PERT CHART THAT TAKES THE LONGEST TIME TO COMPLETE IS THE "CRITICAL PATH" ON YOUR PROJECT.*

Considering the example we did earlier (condensed version below), there are actually three ways (paths) by which we can go from A to H, from beginning to end. We can go A-B-G-H, we can go A-C-D-F-H or A-C-E-F-H. By applying the days required for each activity-line segment in each path, we can determine the critical path.

We've condensed the actual time each of the steps in the chart would take in this simplified version. By adding the segments A-B-G-H, we come up with 81 days. Going A-C-D-F-H totals 93 days, while A-C-E-F-H adds up to 88.

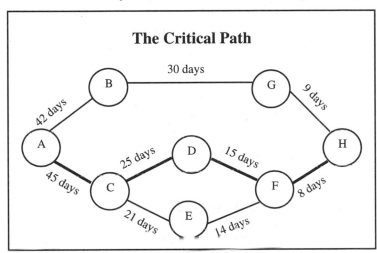

The Critical Path

Therefore, in the illustration, the Critical Path is the A-C-D-F-H — the longest path. We've drawn this line heavier than the others to demonstrate its importance. This is the critical line because we cannot afford to lag behind on this line. Any delay along this line will result in a delay in completion, unless we are able to make up the time later in the project.

If one step along the A-B-G-H path takes a day or two longer than we planned, it's not any real problem, because we had 12 days to spare along this path. However, this doesn't mean we want to intentionally waste any days. If we suddenly found ourselves 13 days behind on the A-B-G-H path, or six days behind on the A-C-E-F-H, it would be a problem. Adding 13 to the original 81 days on A-B-G-H makes 94. Adding six days to the original 88 days on A-C-E-F-H is 94. Either event would mean there is now a different critical path, and the completion date will be pushed back if something isn't done.

The critical path's most important function is to help you establish your priorities. Any activity along the critical path is a high priority. Each day as you complete your 15 minutes of planning, any flow charts associated with your activities need to be present. Determining where you stand along each path enables you to assign true priority rankings to the items on the daily action list.

In developing the critical path, please be realistic: A plan with no cushion is doomed to failure before you begin! Try to allow some extra time, and make your time estimates conservative. Remember, you don't want the plan to control you — you control the plan.

A Separate Critical Path

If we were to begin by drawing out a critical path only (without an existing PERT chart), we would go about it a little differently. The illustration below shows the same activities as the preceding PERT chart drawn in the Critical Path Method:

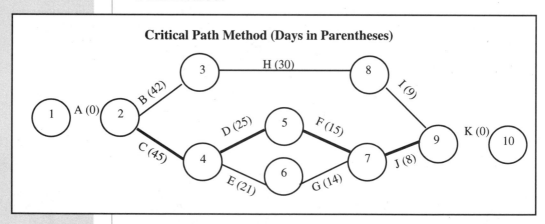

Critical Path Method (Days in Parentheses)

As you can see, the CPM approach puts the greatest emphasis on the process of the activities, rather than on the completion of the activities. In the first illustration of the Ice Hockey Guide plan, the completion events were listed inside the circles, with deadlines and delegations next to the circles.

The lines between the circles represent the particular activity going on, but not yet completed, and we merely added the total number of days between deadlines and indicated them along the lines, to come up with our total days for each path.

In doing only a Critical Path, then, the major focus is on the activities, not their completion, and how much time each step will take. Therefore, the information we need will appear along the lines, not inside the circles. The circles are numbered only for identification of start or finish events, not for the activity itself (the activities, as you see, are lettered). In addition, there is sometimes the appearance of an "instant" activity that takes no time at the merger of various paths along the project.

The GANTT Chart

The GANTT chart, named for its creator, Henry Gantt, also gives us a visual display of activities associated with a project, but presents the information in a different fashion.

Possibly the main weakness of a PERT chart is that the focus is on an activity, rather than a time line. This doesn't mean you can't control time using a PERT chart, but sometimes impending time concerns aren't as clear as you might like them to be. For instance, imagine you're looking at a PERT chart consisting of eight parallel steps at this phase of the project, and today is August 26. How can you identify quickly just what is the most important thing to be working on today? You can usually figure it out, but this is often easier done with a GANTT chart.

The GANTT chart differs from PERT; a GANTT chart is a time line, not an activity line.

Look at the following illustration. As you will see, the GANTT chart is a bar chart in which the separate activities are listed along the left side, with an actual time line across the bottom. This particular project (an office relocation) is planned to take just a little over six weeks to complete.

10

In doing the plan this way, the many steps are listed. Then bar lines are written in, not only to show exactly how much time each step should take, indicated by the length of each line, but also to demonstrate exactly when this step needs to occur, indicated by the position of the line relative to the timeline at the bottom of the graph.

The example here is of a completed chart, because the bars are solidly filled in. When the GANTT chart is begun, the bars are empty rectangles. They are filled in as progress is made.

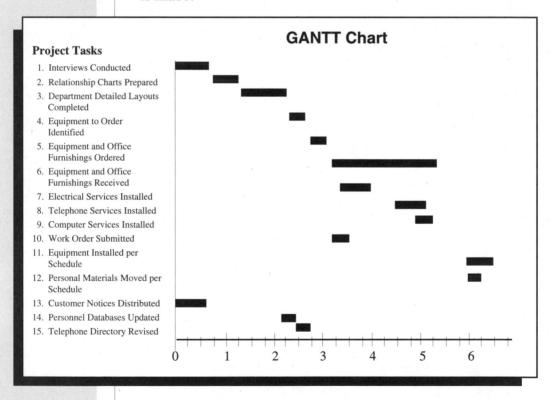

GANTT Chart

Project Tasks

1. Interviews Conducted
2. Relationship Charts Prepared
3. Department Detailed Layouts Completed
4. Equipment to Order Identified
5. Equipment and Office Furnishings Ordered
6. Equipment and Office Furnishings Received
7. Electrical Services Installed
8. Telephone Services Installed
9. Computer Services Installed
10. Work Order Submitted
11. Equipment Installed per Schedule
12. Personal Materials Moved per Schedule
13. Customer Notices Distributed
14. Personnel Databases Updated
15. Telephone Directory Revised

0   1   2   3   4   5   6

You can learn much about how this project has been planned, and how realistically, by considering some of the information on the chart. The first six numbered steps seem to represent a series of events, and one does not start until the

10

previous step is completed. In analyzing further, you'll see this makes perfect sense; after all, you would want to interview people to learn what they wanted before you could determine who needed to be located next to whom in the new office setup for maximum work flow and communications efficiency. You can't order the equipment until you've decided what to order. Actually, these first six steps could also be expressed in a single straight-line PERT chart.

Note a few other important features of the GANTT chart. Step #13 reads "Customer Notices Distributed." As you can see, this is scheduled at the very beginning of the process. You don't have to know what the layout of your new office is going to be to let your customers know you're going to move, your new address, phone number and the anticipated move date. In fact, the sooner they know, the better.

In the middle of the chart are several related steps. A work order is submitted (#10) before the electrician comes in to install electric services (#7). Once electrical services are in, it's possible to install the telephone service (#8). When the phones are in, it is possible to install the computer services (#9).

What if the electrician calls and says that, because another job has taken longer than expected, work in the office can't begin until two days after the scheduled date? Looking at the chart, you see a four-day gap between steps 7 and 8. You can tell the electrician you're still all right, because there is some cushion built into the chart. You might not tell the electrician there are four days, only that you're adding one day to the completion date.

Likewise, at the very end, there is another four-day gap during the sixth week when apparently nothing is scheduled. Great planning! This is to allow for some unexpected delays that still won't affect the actual completion date for the project that, because of the termination of the old lease, might be inflexible.

10

10

By the way, you may not actually want to show this slack time in any external distribution of this flow chart. Work has a tendency to expand to fill the time available, so even though there are four extra days scheduled in here, it may be unwise to show this cushion to others.

With a GANTT chart as part of a daily planning session, you have clear pictures of just where you are on the calendar and where you need to be based on the project you're undertaking. On any given day, the bar lines will be empty, filled or partially filled, depending on what has actually been done. In determining what's the most important priority for the day, it may well be the one that has fallen slightly behind schedule, particularly if the other steps are progressing well.

Once again, the flow chart's visual information helps in decision-making as we plan our day!

The GANTT chart is not without its drawbacks, which is why it's not used as often or as widely as PERT. While it is excellent at demonstrating the time orientation of activities, it simply does not do a very good job of showing how the activities relate to each other in terms of what will precede or follow a specific activity on the chart.

In addition, changes on the GANTT chart are much more difficult to include once the chart has been completed. The effects of missed deadlines or unforeseen activities cannot be easily incorporated. A PERT chart can be easily modified because the dates and time lines are not the critical function of the chart.

Which Chart Should I Use?

Good question! Which one seems to be more comfortable for you? Which chart will better communicate to others the priorities and deadlines? Which one works best for your kind of projects and activities? Perhaps the answer will be both charts. Most project-management software available today is capable of giving us the information in either form. And, depending on who might be using the chart and why, maybe both are better than either one.

Many companies use both charts: a PERT chart in making proposals and selling their clients because it gave such a clear picture for someone outside the daily activity of the project; and the GANTT chart for their internal planning, scheduling and communication.

Summary of Advantages: PERT and GANTT Charts

PERT Chart:

- Clearly shows relationships between activities
- Easily understood by someone outside the project
- Deadlines and delegations can be specifically indicated next to each step
- Critical path may be easily identified and shown for planning and prioritizing

GANTT Chart:

- Timeline at bottom shows relative length of project activities
- Empty bar lines can be filled in to indicate progress to date
- Unscheduled time readily identifiable if needed to be used
- Vertical line representing current date clearly shows potential problems

10

The Simplest Tool of All — The Briefing Board

A very simple — and less precise-tracking mechanism for personal or non-critical job related projects is the briefing board.

A briefing board is mounted on a wall for quick, easy, frequent visibility. This is what a briefing board looks like.

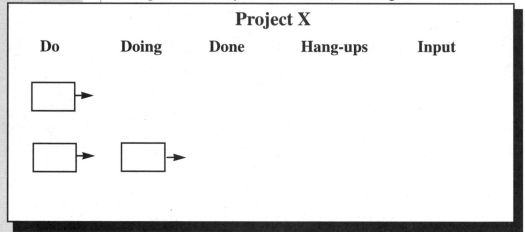

Each header ("Do, Doing, Done, Hang-ups, Inputs") is placed on a separate 5 x 7 card. Under Do, post all the component tasks of the project in question. Post each on a separate 3 x 5 card so they can be moved individually and independently of the others throughout the process.

Once you've planned out the project and posted each Do step, get started. As you begin working on a component, move its card from Do to Doing. Over time, as components are completed, these cards are moved over to Done. At a glance you can see what's yet to be started, what's in process and what's been finished.

Sometimes you'll find a card stays under Do too long. This may indicate you have some type of a hang-up with that step. Maybe you don't know where to start or where to get the necessary information. Take a moment to determine what your hang-up is, write it on a card and post it under Hang-ups in the row with its Do card. Every time you look at the board, your mind will automatically be put to work in search of a solution.

The Inputs column is for your flashes of brilliance that occur at inconvenient times. Suppose you are hard at work on another matter when the solution to your Hang-up pops into your head. Simply jot it on a card, post it under Input and continue with your other work. When time permits, you can go back to the briefing board, pick up your idea and follow through. Input cards could also come from others who have ideas for your project. What a great way to get additional input without rearranging everyone's schedule to have a meeting!

You can use one briefing board to track multiple projects. Simply color code the component cards for easy visual tracking. Or color code the cards according to individual responsibility: John's are blue, Jane's are yellow, etc. Be creative.

The briefing board obviously lacks the precision and sophistication of the other tools presented here, but it can be an extremely valuable addition to your tracking arsenal, especially for personal projects.

10

Murphy's Laws of Project Tracking

To maintain a sense of perspective and humor, keep in mind these Murphy's Laws of project management.

1. Projects progress quickly to a 90 percent completion factor, and then stay at 90 percent forever.

2. When things are going well, something goes wrong.

3. If the content of the project changes often, the rate of change will always overtake the rate of progress.

4. A poorly planned project will take three times longer to complete than expected; a well-planned project only takes twice as long to complete.

5. Members of the project team will ignore your progress reports because the reports portray the limited progress that has been made.

6. When you know you've thought of everything, you haven't.

Making It Work

CONCERN	REASON	STRATEGY
project not in control	project too big	plan and display it using a flow chart
missing activities	overlooked in planning process	think backwards for better concentration and clarity
difficulty with people not finishing jobs by deadline	haven't bought it, don't understand importance	demonstrate with flow chart relationship of activities
activity falls behind schedule	amount of time not properly estimated	with early warning, use flow chart to negotiate changes
constant pressure to finish steps or project	no float time in flow chart	estimate generously, build cushions into time schedule
flow charts messy and disorganized	steps overlooked or not anticipated when planning	complete PERT worksheet before making flow chart
many activities appear to be top priority	true priorities not known	identify Critical Path of project to know priority
difficulty in seeing time relationships of steps	base of PERT chart is not time, but activity line	develop GANTT (bar) chart to better see time connection
people don't respect the timeline	haven't "bought in" yet	make reasonable, equitable suggestions and ask questions for agreement
timeline doesn't work	something is missing	better planning use flow chart
project gets bogged down	something else took top priority on the list	make it top priority again take one of the nine steps
job is held up	lack of materials	accept a partial delivery

10

Summary of Key Points

- Make your timelines specific as to date and time.

- That which can be done anytime is never done at all.

- Timelines will work if they are reasonable, equitable and self-imposed.

- Remember, there is normally more than one right way to do something. Don't let your preconceptions get in the way of your creativity.

- By using flow charts, you will be able to see your options for getting the project back on track.

- Flow charts were devised to keep track of large, multi-step projects involving many people.

- State of the art project tracking software is particularly useful for complex, sophisticated projects. Check the Internet for the latest.

- Thinking backwards is a more effective planning process when using a PERT chart.

- In thinking backwards, always identify the activity or activities that must be completed prior to the beginning of the activity in consideration.

- Include dates and delegations in your PERT chart, so that all relevant information will be on display in the chart.

- Use flow chart information to negotiate for schedule changes or for more assistance.

- Complete a PERT worksheet prior to drawing out your PERT chart for maximum clarity and neatness in the finished diagram.

10

- Count the number of days required for each possible path from beginning to end of your PERT chart to determine the critical path for your project.

- Always make activities along your critical path top priority.

- In determining time frames for each activity, estimate conservatively to allow for some cushion if unexpected events slow you down.

- Use a GANTT chart to show the time relationships of activities in your plan.

- Study your flow charts after a project has been completed to learn how to plan the activity more accurately the next time you do it.

- A briefing board is an excellent tracking tool for simpler professional projects and for personal/family projects as well.

10

Putting Timelines, Deadlines and Project Tracking to Work in Your Life

WORKSHEET — Project Timelines

Directions: Select a project you're currently working on or one you've completed, but which didn't go as well as you'd hoped and answer the following questions about it.

1. How can I minimize this project? What could I subtract or shorten?

2. What could I change about my plan? By adding or duplicating or extending a timeline, what might happen?

3. Can I rearrange anything here? Are the sequences, the people involved, or the steps inflexible, or is there some flexibility?

4. What substitutions would make this project work even better? Take even less time?

5. What other ways can I use the time, materials, ideas and energy going into this project?

6. How many different ways could this project be accomplished?

10

Practice Your Flow-Charting Skills

1. **PERT — Personal Project.** Using the blank form below, think of a project you recently completed, or need to finish, that represents basically a single straight line of steps that you have control over. Try to think of a small project, with six or fewer steps. Work from right to left, just like we did, and determine in each case what had to happen first before your next step could be taken. Estimate some timelines here and indicate the names for any delegated tasks. It's not important that you use all six circles; just use whatever you need.

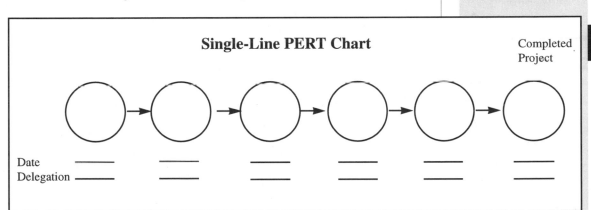

Single-Line PERT Chart

Completed Project

10

Date
Delegation

2. Complete the following exercise to check your understanding of the CPM.

   The chart shows a list of lettered but unnamed activities, the activity or activities that must precede each step, and the days required to complete each. Draw out a critical path, using circles as the start and stop points for each activity and eventually numbering them. Label the activity lines between the circles with the letters above, being aware of the activity or activities that must precede each step. Indicate the number of days required for each activity next to the letter along the activity line.

ACTIVITY	PRECEDING ACTIVITY	DAYS
A	-	0 (start)
B	A	4
C	A	5
D	A	3
E	D	2
F	C	3
G	E	2
H	B	7
I	H	4
J	F, C	3
K	I, J	0

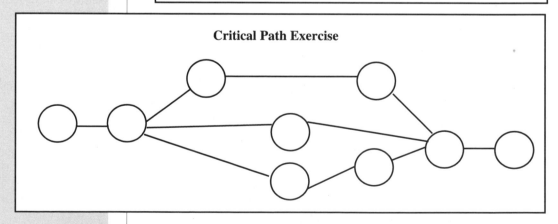

Critical Path Exercise

When you have finished, determine what the critical path is for this project, and how many days it will take. Also, determine how many "cushion" days you have when following other paths. You'll find the answer to this problem at the end of the chapter.

3. To celebrate the birthday of a friend, you have decided to host a dinner in her honor on Saturday night, dinner to be served at 7 p.m. Because you want the gathering to be relaxed and informal, the main course for dinner will be spaghetti. It is now 10 a.m. on Monday.

   Develop either a PERT or GANTT chart to plan this event. Do a PERT worksheet first to identify all the steps required, how long each will take or how much lead time you must allow. At this point no one has been invited. The menu isn't finalized, and you haven't looked in your pantry recently. You want to do something special for the honored guest. Every activity will center upon precisely 7 p.m. Saturday, when at that moment, everyone will sit down and you will serve the now-prepared food. The hot food is hot and the cold food is cold. Good luck!

Action TNT — Today Not Tomorrow
No one ever built a reputation based on what they were going to do tomorrow.

10

MY SLIGHT-EDGE IDEAS
FROM CHAPTER 10:

Answer To Critical Path Problem:

The critical path runs A-B-H-I-K and takes 15 days to complete. Path A-C-F-J-K requires 11 days (four days of cushion). Path A-D-E-G-J-K will take 10 days to complete (with five extra days). See illustration below.

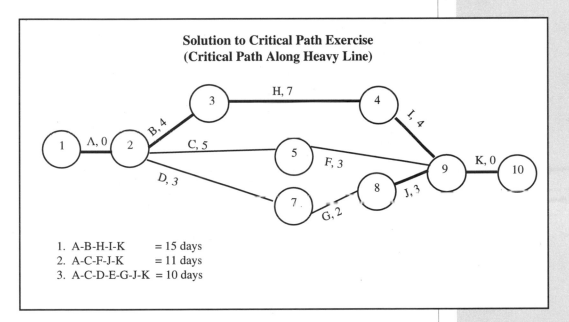

Solution to Critical Path Exercise
(Critical Path Along Heavy Line)

1. A-B-H-I-K   = 15 days
2. A-C-F-J-K   = 11 days
3. A-C-D-E-G-J-K = 10 days

10

Spaghetti Dinner Exercise

There are many factors that may have become a part of your flow chart. Of course, there are no right or wrong answers, but if something was overlooked, it could prove embarrassing or detrimental to the atmosphere of the evening. Here are a few questions to check how thoroughly your evening was planned:

- Did you consider projects not specifically related to the meal itself, but very important to the success of the evening, such as cleaning the house and getting dressed?

- Did you remember: To set the table? To start water boiling for the spaghetti?

- If it's after dark, did you turn on the outside lights?

- Did you consider seating assignments?

- How will you serve the meal: Family style? Buffet style? Restaurant style?

- Did you decide to have background music? Did you select the music you'll play? Did you turn on the equipment?

- Do you have candles and matches for the birthday cake?

- Is the birthday present wrapped? Is the card signed?

CHAPTER 11

Coping With Crisis and Conflict

"Tough times never last ... tough people do."

Robert Schuller

There's not a single idea in this entire manual that is guaranteed to work 100 percent of the time! Crises happen; that's a fact of life. Remember Murphy's Laws:

> ### *IF ANYTHING CAN GO WRONG, IT WILL.*

> ### *NOTHING IS AS EASY AS IT LOOKS.*

> ### *EVERYTHING TAKES LONGER THAN YOU THINK.*

> ### *LEFT TO THEMSELVES,*
> ### *THINGS TEND TO GO FROM BAD TO WORSE.*

> ### *IF THERE IS A POSSIBILITY OF SEVERAL THINGS GOING WRONG, THE ONE THAT WILL CAUSE THE MOST DAMAGE WILL BE THE ONE THAT GOES WRONG.*

11

MURPHY IS AN OPTIMIST.

Despite being whimsical statements, each of Murphy's Laws contains a substantial element of truth. Everyone has experienced things similar enough to the situations they portray to find a great amount of personal identification with each law.

It's inevitable when organizing and managing multiple priorities and projects, that everything won't go according to plan. Sometimes the most unexpected event works its way into the project. And the best crisis-prevention technique you have is to keep an eye out for one of Murphy's Laws to appear and to be prepared for it.

Conflict and crisis are often necessary to keep things on track, encourage integrative solutions and recognize potential problems. How you manage the process will determine how effectively you use the energy stemming from crisis.

Collected research from priority management indicates that crisis and conflict happen most frequently in these areas, in this order:

- Schedules

- Project priorities

- Human resources

- Technical options and performance trade-offs

- Administrative procedures

- Personality and behavior

- Cost

You need to be ready and you must have the right attitude. Effective crisis management is essential for project success. Neglect, avoidance and denial only doom your efforts to ultimate failure.

11

Assessment: Are You Ready for Crisis?

Directions:

Time to see where you stand on preparedness! Read the following statements and circle the number that best indicates whether you (3) agree; (2) are not sure; (1) disagree.

	Agree	Unsure	Disagree
1. I know my department's most vulnerable areas.	3	2	1
2. If I got into a real bind, several people would help me out.	3	2	1
3. I have a written contingency plan for my worst nightmare.	3	2	1
4. I already use flow charts to track my projects.	3	2	1
5. I learned a valuable lesson from my last mistake.	3	2	1
6. I tend to avoid others if the potential for conflict exists.	3	2	1
7. I welcome conflicts and crises on my job.	3	2	1
8. When things go wrong, I can always keep control.	3	2	1
9. I can be very flexible when change needs to occur.	3	2	1

11

What it means:

22 or more:	Emergency? You're prepared!
21 - 14:	You're holding back water, but the dike is leaking
less than 14:	Did you know your building is on fire?

Contingency Planning

Preparation for crisis begins simply with a plan for what you are going to do if and when something unexpected does occur. Remember the story about Johnson & Johnson and that company's quick and effective response to the Tylenol scare? That's an excellent example of a company being prepared and having a plan to implement immediately.

An example of not being prepared was the Exxon tanker at Valdez, Alaska, which ran aground resulting in one of the largest oil spills in history. Not only was the company not ready, neither the city nor the state governments of the area had much to brag about in terms of emergency readiness. The irony of the Exxon oil spill tragedy was that there *once had been a contingency plan* in place. The equipment was there, and the people were trained and ready. But it was decided that a spill of this enormity really couldn't happen, so the workers and equipment so vital to preventing disaster were sent elsewhere.

Lesson: BE READY FOR ANYTHING!

1. **What is likely to go wrong?** To be ready for disaster, you must identify where you might be the most vulnerable. Imagine a worst-case scenario, and ask: Can I live with this? What is the likelihood of this happening? Your challenge is to establish techniques for discovering problems before they become crises.

   To meet this challenge, remember the feedback system from Chapter 3 — the FAR way: Feedback, Appraisal and Revision. Being aware of and open to this process creates an atmosphere of openness, honesty and fairness among your project team. With an effective team-member feedback system in place, you will have the information necessary for anticipating problems.

2. **When will you know about it?** Obviously, the sooner the better. Your challenge is to have systems in place that properly communicate project status. This is the real plus of flow charts like PERT and GANTT. These tools are capable of giving you the early warning critical to surviving the crises.

   Establish guidelines for proper reporting so the first signs of a problem are quickly visible.

   • Schedule weekly or regular team meetings. Circulate the agenda in advance.

   • Use charts whenever possible, and make them visually available to the people working with you.

   • Put goals, procedures and expectations in writing.

   • Make this a positive information reporting system — not a cause for discipline or reprimanding. Don't shoot the messenger.

   • Watch for developing trends.

11

3. **What will you do?** You must have a plan and be prepared to make immediate decisions.

   • Have backups already in mind. Think and prepare your basic resources of money, machines, materials and human resources.

   • At the earliest point of detection, immediately re-schedule those tasks likely to be involved in the crisis.

   • Be sure your decisions can be justified.

   • Know the objective — the driving factor of the project.

   • Gather facts from the people most directly affected by the situation.

Eight Steps to Crisis Survival

Here is an eight-step survival plan that affords you the necessary persistence, openness, wisdom, energy and responsive action for those times you hope never happen.

1. **Step back and collect your thoughts.** It's imperative you see the big picture, and see it as quickly as possible. Try to assume the role of an outside consultant, someone brought in to solve the problem. If you can see what's really going on in a detached, objective way, the necessary action will become more clear. Try to view the crisis as if it were happening to someone else.

2. **Clear the deck.** Take the minutes necessary to create a workable, productive environment for taking action. Removing the clutter from your desk helps sharpen your focus.

3. **Control or reduce interruptions.** What can you do to avoid as many distractions as possible? Is there a secluded spot in your office or elsewhere where you

can retreat? Can you divert your calls or your visitors to somebody else?

4. **Clarify priorities and deadlines.** Immediately determine if the deadline creating the crisis is a true deadline or simply one that would be nice. Maybe you don't have a crisis after all. If you do, it's time to redouble your efforts. What else is important? Reassign other priority projects to someone else.

5. **Stay focused and work on one thing at a time.** Concentrate your energy on the first task. Stick with it until it's completed. Then you can focus your attention on the next one.

6. **Ask for help!** This is not the time to be the Lone Ranger of priorities. Remember that connectedness is vital to reaching your goals. Ask for any assistance you can get, and use it!

7. **"This, too, shall pass."** This is a handy phrase to keep in the forefront of your mind during a crisis. No matter how bad it may be, eventually you will get through it. You have before, and you will again.

8. **Learn from it!** In the charred ruins of the worst disaster can be found seeds of future success. What kind of learning experience has this disaster given you? Did you learn something you need to do next time to keep it from happening again? Was there something you did that you shouldn't have? What new insight will make you better able to cope with the next experience? History can be an excellent teacher — if you remember to use it.

In the early growth days of IBM, when Tom Watson, Sr., was still head of his little business machine company that was on its way to becoming a corporate giant, one of Watson's most trusted associates, a vice president, made a judgment error that was so bad it cost the company 10 million dollars.

11

Can you imagine making a 10-million dollar mistake? How could you live with it? What would you do? Many of us would do just like this humiliated vice president did. He went into Watson's office, closed the door and said: "I think I had better resign before you fire me."

Watson stared at his associate in disbelief. "Resign?" he thundered. "Fire you? We can't afford to do that. We have just invested 10 million dollars in your education!"

What a great attitude toward disaster. The past is past. You can't go back and change it. You can only learn from it, and you had sure better hope you learned something!

The Chinese symbol for crisis is actually two symbols together: the symbol for danger and the symbol for opportunity. As crisis closes in, try to look beyond the danger and see the window of opportunity behind it.

Two examples: When Johnson & Johnson was dealing with the Tylenol scare, a large toll-free telephone network was quickly established as a crisis hotline for people with concerns, questions and information. The crisis passed but the system remained.

In the years that have followed, that system has been used many other times when quick and far-reaching communications capability was required. When Hurricane Hugo's devastating winds pounded the Atlantic seaboard in 1990, Johnson & Johnson opened up that same toll-free system as a public service to enable emergency communication to take place.

Individual lives and careers are often positively affected by crisis, as well. That no more deaths occurred during the October, 1989 earthquake in Northern California than what did occur is a tribute to fantastic contingency planning by the many governments and municipalities in that area. Exactly 30 days after the quake, the Bay Bridge was reopened. The newscasts all contained much reflecting on the events of the month, and it was amazing to see how some people's lives

11

and careers had reached new levels of achievement due to the opportunity the earthquake provided for them to demonstrate their ability to perform in crisis situations.

Where's the "seed of benefit" in the crisis you're enduring? Keep looking — it's there. And the opportunity and lesson may even make it worth the pain of the crisis.

Dealing With Conflict

One difference between crisis and conflict is this: Crisis involves activities. Conflict involves people. All of us have conflicts with ourselves, with other people, and with the organizations we work with. Conflict, like crisis, can throw our best planned projects onto the scrap heap.

The emotional and stress level of conflict is likely to be much higher that that in a crisis because people take conflict so personally. Psychologists say that people cope with conflict in six basic ways:

1. They back off.
2. They become indifferent to the situation.
3. They make concessions.
4. They use a third party for counsel.
5. They establish the "enemy" position.
6. They problem-solve.

You can look at this list and quickly see methods that are productive. Also, you can see how a combination of methods might be useful. *You can't always control what happens to you, but you can control how you deal with it.* Make a plan involving what you can control and leaving out what you can't control. In your survival plan, consider the following:

11

1. **Accept the situation.** Keep your cool. Conflict happens. As the late Malcolm Forbes, publisher of Forbes magazine, once said, "A job without conflict is a hobby." How true! Do you know anyone with a job involving worth with other people who has no conflict at all? The more responsibility you have, the higher the likelihood of conflict. Your value to your organization and to yourself increases in direct proportion to how effectively you can manage the conflict of your job and your life.

2. **Assess the situation.** Ask yourself, "What is the real problem here?" Frequently what appears to be the problem in a conflict is only a symptom of something else underlying the reactions. Is something in this situation pushing one of your hot buttons? Are you overreacting? Is this really a big deal in the overall scheme of things? Look at the big picture. Analyze. Look deeply. Ask someone else for their view.

3. **Focus on areas of agreement.** Most people focus instead on the disagreements, accentuating those areas and polarizing their positions. Stay focused on the goal of getting the task accomplished. Creating a common ground and enlarging your areas of agreement is vital.

4. **Think Win/Win.** Look for solutions beneficial to both sides. Work in a spirit of cooperation and avoid taking an adversarial role. Control your need to be right.

5. **Be tough on the facts, but go easy on the people.** Are you taking the conflict personally? Try to distance yourself emotionally. Damaging a relationship will only make matters worse, both now and for the future.

6. **Negotiate ... Cooperate ... Compromise.** How many different ways could this conflict possibly be solved? Brainstorm for ideas. Consider even those that seem a little far-fetched. Then discuss them directly with all involved.

7. **Commit to a course of action.** You may still disagree on various points but commit anyway once the decision has been made. This may be one of those instances when you must agree to disagree. Accept the final decision, commit to it, and implement it.

8. **Monitor and modify.** Resolving a conflict can be like driving a car down the road. You choose a direction and set off. But if you don't adjust your steering to match the turns in the road, you'll end up in the ditch. Likewise, your conflict resolution plan requires constant guidance and modification to keep it on track.

11

Making It Work

CONCERN	REASON	STRATEGY
not knowing what might happen	haven't thought about it	develop a worst-case scenario
lack of cooperation	team concept not implemented	have regular meeting with positive orientation
problem sneaking up on me	visual aids not available or not working	develop flow charts and update frequently
being too subjective	too close to situation	become a "consultant"
losing focus during crisis	doing too many things at once	pick one activity, work on it until completed
mentally or emotionally overwhelmed	taking problem too seriously	"This too shall pass" — recall past experiences
tend to ignore crisis	see as negative situation	look for learning benefit
many conflicts with others	dealing with symptoms focusing on differences	look for real problem identify areas of agreement
avoidance of conflicts	dislike negative emotions take conflicts personally	expect conflict as natural, distance self emotionally
loss of control, loss of temper	try to control everything, actually believe I can	identify what you can/can't do, use to your benefit

11

Summary of Key Points

- How you deal with conflicts and crises is more important than what happens to you.

- Recognizing the truth of Murphy's Laws gives you a healthy mindset toward crisis.

- With a good contingency plan, you can be ready for anything!

- Flow charts and regular reporting will establish early warning of potential problem areas.

- Put yourself in a consultant's role as you objectively observe conflicts and crises to determine what is happening and why.

- Work on one thing until you have completed it. Then tackle another.

- Don't be too proud to ask for help when things go wrong.

- Look for the seeds of benefit and the lesson to be learned in every crisis.

- Acknowledge conflict as a necessary part of your job: It's what you're being paid for.

- Welcome disagreement as a chance to exchange ideas and look at a situation from another's perspective.

11

Putting Crisis and Conflict Management to Work in Your Life

1. Review the last crisis you handled. What could you have done differently? What is your plan for next time?

2. Prepare a contingency plan for one of your current projects. Be sure to cover all the bases and to be prepared for anything.

3. Do you take conflict personally? What steps could you take as a conflict arises to distance yourself emotionally?

4. Who are the people you are in conflict with most often? What can you do to reduce the tensions between you?

5. Chart a 30-day course of action. Reassess your progress in 30 days and modify your plan.

Action TNT — Today Not Tomorrow

No one ever built a reputation based on what they were going to do tomorrow.

11

MY SLIGHT-EDGE IDEAS
ABOUT CRISIS AND CONFLICT:

11

11

C HAPTER 12

Life Balance

"Life is not measured by the breaths you take, but by its breathtaking moments."

                                                    Michael Vance

---

Many smart business people work hard, reach for the stars, and feel oddly ambivalent about their success. They want to slow down. The don't want to stay over-stretched and over-stressed, but they lack the commitment to get started.

Simplicity specialist Elaine St. James explains:

"It takes time to make time. You can't figure out how to create time for the things you enjoy if you don't take time to rethink what you're doing now. Maintaining a complicated life is a great way to avoid changing it."

You can't measure how effectively you manage the priorities and activities of life when you're looking only at your career ... unless all that matters to you is that career. Most of the time, however, we're too busy being busy to think about the elements of a balanced and happy life. Take a break from the hectic pace of your life and complete these assessments.

12

Assessment: How Big Is the Gap Between What You Want and What You Do?

Rate the following four items in order of importance to you. Use 1 for the most important, 4 for the least.

Importance _____ _____ _____ _____

Family   Work   Leisure   Spiritual,
                     Activities   character

Time Spent _____ _____ _____ _____

Rate them again based on the *amount of time* you spend on each. Use 1 for the most time consuming, 4 for the least.

Do your rankings match? If not, do the discrepancies explain some of the inner conflict and turmoil you feel? What choices can you make to move your rankings closer together?

Everything you do in life is a choice. Everything. You may not like your choices, but you can and do make choices constantly. And you must recognize that they are *your* choices ... not anyone else's.

Suppose you had made plans to take your son fishing. This was a big event for the two of you and you had planned for it for months. At the last minute, your company announced a mandatory training seminar that directly conflicted with your fishing trip. Everyone in the organization was required to attend. Do you have any choice here?

Contrary to popular belief, you do have choices. You could choose to attend the training seminar and break your commitment to your son and accept the potential for damage to your relationship. Or you could choose to tell your boss that you cannot attend the seminar because of a prior commitment and accept the potential consequences of not complying with the company's request for your attendance at the program. Perhaps neither choice is an ideal one but you must make the choice that's best for you, the one with the least objectionable consequences to you.

Assessment: How's Your Balance?

The balance wheel represents six critical areas of life. Rate your satisfaction and success in each area of your life. The inner circle represents a 1 (great dissatisfaction) and the outer end of the line represents a 10 (great satisfaction). Mark each spoke based on where you are along that continuum.

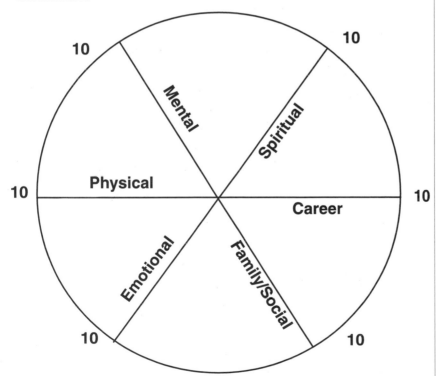

Career

- How would you rate yourself in your career?
- Are you satisfied with what you've achieved, your professional respect, your responsibilities, your income?
- Do you enjoy your work?
- Are you fairly good at it?

Place a mark on the career line between 1 (the center circle) and 10.

Spiritual

- Do you have a sense of inner peace?
- Are you comfortable with your place in the universe?

Rate yourself here, 1 - 10.

Mental

- Are you still learning? Do you seek new ideas? Develop new interests?
- Are you challenging your mind and thought processes in ways different from the old ones?
- Had a class recently? Read any good books lately?
- How mentally and intellectually stimulated are you?

Place a mark on the mental line between 1 and 10.

Physical

- Are you taking care of your body? Exercising it intelligently?
- Have you seen a doctor for a physical check-up lately?
- What have you been putting into your body recently? Quantity and quality food? Caffeine? Alcohol? Nicotine? Narcotics? What is the status of your health? Are you satisfied with your weight?

- Are you getting your body to bed at a reasonable hour?

Place a mark on the physical line between 1 and 10.

Emotional

- Are you truly happy?
- Do you have trouble getting up each morning to face another day of your life?
- Do you suffer from depression?
- Where's your anger and frustration threshold? How short is your fuse?

Place a mark on the emotional line between 1 and 10.

Family/Social

- When was the last time you considered putting a real effort in this area? Or are you just too busy?
- If you're married, are you delivering in marriage what you promised in courtship?
- Got a good close friend or two you could count on in any situation?
- If you're a parent, how did you celebrate your children's past birthdays? Valentine's Day?

Be honest. This is just for you. Lowest is 1, 10 is tops.

Now connect the dots around your balance wheel. This wheel of life is designed to take you smoothly toward your destination. Are you living a well-rounded life or do you have a serious imbalance to take care of? If it's a wheel, what does it look like? Do you have a flat tire? Are you in for a very bumpy ride? Now you know why your life goes topsy-turvy every now and then.

Now that you know the "shape" of your life, you can take steps to smooth out the rough spots. Did you have an area or two that are much weaker than the others? If so, these are areas that you might consider devoting additional

12

time, effort and attention to developing to your satisfaction. Make a list of actions you could take in each area that would move you in the direction you want to go. Then do a priority grid with these items to help you determine where to start.

Note: If you have some areas that are very high and others that are very low, you may have to give up some things in the high areas in order to have the resources necessary to improve other areas. For instance, if career is high and family/social is low, a shift in your time allocation may be necessary. That may mean choosing to slow down on your career advancement in order to enhance your family life. But if you choose to do nothing, you need to know that you've chosen to accept your life as it is — you can't expect anything to change unless you're willing to put some effort into making the change happen. There are no right and wrong choices. Only those that are appropriate for you. Do not allow anyone else to tell you what your choices should be. Do not succumb to the "social mirror" of other people's perspective or expectations of you.

Did you know that:

- Colonel Sanders was "too old" to start a business?

- Fred Astaire's first screen test stated: "Can't act! Slightly bald! Can dance a little."?

- Florence Chadwick knew that other people had died trying to swim across the English Channel?

Had these people given up because someone else had said their efforts were doomed to failure, they'd never have succeeded. But each believed in himself or herself. So must you believe in yourself, because you're the only one that can effect real change in your life.

The shape of your balance wheel also tends to be indicative of your overall stress level. Poor balance = high stress. Modern mankind in general shows numerous signs of chronic stress overload. How many of these signs apply to you?

12

Assessment: Stress Level

Symptoms of Chronic Stress Overload				
	YES	**NO**	**YES**	**NO**
Problems in home/work life			Inability to let go of past mistakes	
Sexual dysfunction			Chronic colds/flu/infections, etc.	
Ulcers/Diarrhea			High blood pressure/heart attack/stroke	
Indigestion/Vomiting			Rapid emotional swings	
Insomnia and other sleep disorders			Headache/Backache/Muscle aches	
Depression/Anxiety			Chronic fatigue	
Drug/Alcohol abuse			Inability to function/Mental fatigue	
Increased smoking			Worsening of PMS/Menstrual irregularity	
Compulsive behaviors			Increased cholesterol levels	
Irritability/tension			Infertility problems	
Passive-Aggressive behavior			Impulsive behavior	
Misjudging motives			Mouth dryness	
Procrastination			Loss of perspective	
Appetite changes/Eating disorders			Forgetfulness	
Confusion				

12

311

Exactly what is stress and where does it all come from? Stress is the neurological and hormonal response of the human body to any of the demands placed upon it. Adrenaline and other body chemicals build up and must be released. It comes from overcommitment. It comes from setting your expectations too high. It comes from not having enough goals or having incompatible goals. It comes from trying to meet everyone else's expectations in addition to your own. It comes from striving, seeking, searching for success and for meaning in life.

Stress comes from searching for ways to have it all, to do it all, all at once.

> *YOU CANNOT HAVE IT ALL —*
> *AT LEAST NOT AT THE SAME TIME!*
> *CHOICES MUST BE MADE.*

12

Holmes Stress Scale —
Life changes are listed in order of resulting stress

Death of a spouse	100	Change in responsibility at work	29
Divorce	73	Son or daughter leaving home	29
Marital separation	65	Trouble with in-laws	29
Jail term	63	Outstanding personal achievement	28
Death of close relative	63	Spouse starting/stopping work	26
Personal injury or illness	53	Beginning or ending school	26
Marriage	50	Revision of personal habits	24
Fired from job	47	Trouble with boss	23
Marital reconciliation	45	Change in working hours	20
Retirement	45	Change in working conditions	20
Change in health, family	44	Change in residence	20
Pregnancy	40	Change in school	20
Sexual differences	39	Change in recreation	19
Gain of new family member	39	Change in social activities	18
Change in financial status	38	Loan	17
Death of a close friend	37	Change in sleeping habits	16
Change of new line of work	36	Change in family get-togethers	15
Argument with spouse	35	Change in eating habits	15
Mortgage	31	Vacation	13
Foreclosure of mortgage	30	Minor violations of the law	11

12

Action Steps to Control Stress

The key to managing stress and preventing burnout is to follow a regular routine for managing stress before it builds to explosive levels. Here's a list of tips, tactics, and time-tested techniques to attack the root causes of stress, not just the symptoms.

- **Realign what you want with what you do.** Strive for balance.

- **Make time to reboot.** Get up a few minutes earlier to give yourself time to relax, contemplate and mentally prepare yourself for the day. Use your evening commuting time to decompress and shift gears from work to home.

- **Leave your work at work.** Easier said than done, but nonetheless essential. Envision a tree right outside your home. Each evening, hang your briefcase and work thoughts on that tree to clear your mind for the evening. In the morning, take the work back off the tree on your way to work. Faithfully doing your 15 minutes of planning before leaving the office will help a great deal.

- **Free up one hour a day for 30 days.** It won't be easy, but just do it. Use that time to reflect and answer these questions: Do you like your job? Are you working too hard? Are your kids draining all your energy? Is your marriage working?

- **Less is more.** Scale back. You can work fewer hours without losing any productivity by using the tips and techniques in this manual. Get rid of the clutter of your life. Go through your house once a year and get rid of all the stuff you haven't used in the past 12 months. Remove anything that doesn't add fullness to your life. Most of the stuff is just that ... stuff that simply gets in the way and creates maintenance hassles. Develop the self-discipline not to replace the stuff you dispose. If you really want to scale back, move to a smaller house. Remember, stuff expands to fill the space available.

- **Just say no, no, no.** Playwright Jules Renard wrote, "The truly free man is he who can decline a dinner invitation without giving an excuse." You can't simplify your life if you can't say no. The more you say it, the easier it gets. And the more you say no, the less people will ask you in the first place!

- **Maintain only three priorities at a time.** Work is obviously one unless you work for the fun of it. For most people, family is another. That leaves only one more. Maybe for you it is staying in shape. Maybe it is church work. Maybe it is gardening. Figure out what really matters to you the most and refrain from committing to other areas. Remember, the hardest choices are not between things you want to do and things you don't. They're among all the things that interest you. Overcommitting complicates your life.

- **Develop a support network.** Like the Canada geese, we truly do need each other. Do you have a support network, some kind of advisory group that can give you encouragement and energy? If not, why not put such a group together? It could be some of your friends or associates who might also benefit from the mutual sharing of ideas and support.

- **Assert yourself.** Say what you need and ask for what you want.

- **Take care of your body.** Build energy and balance through proper nutrition, moderate exercise and good health care.

- **Lighten up.** Keep a sense of humor and perspective. When things get crazy, get goofy.

12

- **Keep your commitment to your commitment.**
- **Love life and life will love you back.**

Just as you can't have it all at once, don't try to make all your changes at once. Take it one step at a time. Commit to a plan and do it. Reassess periodically to ensure you're still on track.

Achieving balance — or even approaching it — takes time. Most of the really worthwhile things in life do.

Making It Work

CONCERN	REASON	STRATEGY
Life out of balance; chronic high stress	Lack of focus; overcommitment; unrealistic expectations; no support network	Realign what you do with what you want; learn to say no and to ask for what you want; redefine your own expectations and priorities; put network in place

Summary of Key Points

- Balance must be sought among life's six arenas: career, physical, mental, emotional, spiritual, and family/social.

- How you live your life is your choice and your choice alone. Other people's expectations are irrelevant.

- You cannot have it all, do it all, at least not all at once.

- Chronic stress is epidemic.

- Limit priorities to three. Learn to say no.

- Learn to leave work at work.

- Develop a support network and ask for what you want.

- Achieving balance takes time.

Putting Balance in Your Life

1. What do you want most out of life?

2. Why don't you already have it? What would it take to get it?

3. What do you want more of in your life?

4. What do you want less of?

5. Complete all the assessments in this chapter and chart a 30-day course of action. Reassess your progress in 30 days and modify your plan.

12

Action TNT — Today Not Tomorrow

No one ever built a reputation based on what they were going to do tomorrow.

MY SLIGHT-EDGE IDEAS
ABOUT LIFE BALANCE:

*I*NDEX

80-20 rule   23-25, 28-29, 48, 128

A

appointments   81, 83, 100, 113, 194, 201
appraisal   44-45, 293
assessments   305, 317

B

briefing board   276-277, 281

C

calendar   14, 65, 77, 79, 81-83, 85, 88, 100, 104, 113,
    115, 118, 126, 151, 157, 161, 176, 233, 274
commitment   5, 7, 12-13, 17-18, 36, 39, 47, 87, 98,
    100, 107-108, 127-128, 137-140, 143, 146, 152, 168,
    173, 182, 186, 201, 211, 222, 231, 234, 247, 250,
    305, 307, 316
communication   9, 39, 162, 187, 196, 203, 213-214,
    217-218, 222-224, 227, 230-231, 238, 240-242, 254,
    275, 296
computer
    devices   88-90, 93
    software   86-87, 89, 256-257, 261, 274, 280
conflict   172, 212, 218, 222, 228-230, 289-291, 293,
    295, 297-303, 306

I

in-between time   25-26, 29, 117, 157, 160, 163

interruptions

    boss   35, 129, 139, 159, 164, 198, 212, 222-230, 235, 240-241, 307, 313

    drop-ins   192-194

    visitors   192, 196, 206, 295

    voice mail   77, 198-199, 202-205, 208-209

K

key functions   101-102, 128-129

L

lists

    daily action   8-9, 27, 65, 82-84, 91-92, 97, 117, 119-122, 127, 133, 218, 224-226, 240, 270

    master   14, 48, 65, 82-84, 90, 92, 157, 159, 176, 211, 255

    next action   14, 27, 85, 88, 92

    project   65, 83, 85, 119, 129, 215, 236, 267, 271

    someday/maybe   14, 85, 92

    waiting   14, 27, 85, 92, 163, 176

M

measurements   44, 127

meetings

    agendas   157-158, 183-186, 188, 190-191, 207-208, 293

    Eight-Minute   194, 224, 233

    planning guide   183-184, 188-189

mission statements   8, 46, 51, 53, 59-60, 222

O

P

S

T

U

YOUR BACK-OF-THE-BOOK STORE

Because you already know the value of National Press Publications Desktop Handbooks and Business User's Manuals, here's a time-saving way to purchase more career-building resources from our convenient "book store."

- IT'S EASY … Just make your selections, then mail, call or fax us your order. (See back for details.)
- INCREASE YOUR EFFECTIVENESS … Books in these two series have sold more than a million copies and are known as reliable sources of instantly helpful information.
- THEY'RE CONVENIENT TO USE … Each handbook is durable, concise and made of quality materials that will last you all the way to the boardroom.
- YOUR SATISFACTION IS 100% GUARANTEED. Forever.

60-MINUTE TRAINING SERIES™ HANDBOOKS

TITLE	YOUR PRICE*	QTY.	TOTAL
8 Steps for Highly Effective Negotiations #424	$14.95		
Assertiveness #4422	$14.95		
Balancing Career and Family #415	$14.95		
Diversity: Managing Our Differences #412	$14.95		
Dynamic Communication Skills for Women #417	$14.95		
Exceptional Customer Service #4882	$14.95		
Fear & Anger: Control Your Emotions #4302	$14.95		
Getting Things Done #4112	$14.95		
How to Coach an Effective Team #4308	$14.95		
How to Conduct Win-Win Perf. Appraisals #423	$14.95		
How to De-Junk Your Life #4306	$14.95		
How to Handle Conflict and Confrontation #4952	$14.95		
How to Manage Your Boss #493	$14.95		
How to Supervise People #4102	$14.95		
How to Work With People #4032	$14.95		
Listen Up: Hear What's Really Being Said #4172	$14.95		
Motivation and Goal-Setting #4962	$14.95		
A New Attitude #4432	$14.95		
Parenting: Ward & June… #486	$14.95		
The Polished Professional #426	$14.95		
The Power of Innovative Thinking #428	$14.95		
The Power of Self-Managed Teams #4222	$14.95		
Powerful Communication Skills #4132	$14.95		
Powerful Leadership Skills for Women #463	$14.95		
Present With Confidence #4612	$14.95		
The Secret to Developing Peak Performers #4962	$14.95		
Self-Esteem: The Power to Be Your Best #4642	$14.95		
SELF Profile #403	$14.95		
Shortcuts to Organized Files and Records #4307	$14.95		
The Stress Management Handbook #4842	$14.95		
Supreme Teams: How to Make Teams Work #4303	$14.95		
Techniques to Improve Your Writing Skills #460	$14.95		
Thriving on Change #4212	$14.95		
The Write Stuff #414	$14.95		

TITLE	RETAIL PRICE	YOUR PRICE	QTY.	TOTAL
The Assertive Advantage #439	$26.95	$22.95		
Being OK Just Isn't Enough #5407	$26.95	$22.95		
Business Letters for Busy People #449	$26.95	$22.95		
Coping With Difficult People #465	$26.95	$22.95		
Dealing with Conflict and Anger #5402	$26.95	$22.95		
Hand-Picked: Finding & Hiring… #5405	$26.95	$22.95		
High-Impact Presentation and Training Skills #438	$26.95	$22.95		
Learn to Listen #446	$26.95	$22.95		
Lifeplanning #476	$26.95	$22.95		
The Manager's Role as Coach #456	$26.95	$22.95		
The Memory System #452	$26.95	$22.95		
Negaholics® No More #5406	$26.95	$22.95		
Parenting the Other Chick's Eggs #5404	$26.95	$22.95		
Taking AIM On Leadership #5401	$26.95	$22.95		
Prioritize, Organize: Art of Getting It Done 2nd ed. #4532	$26.95	$22.95		
The Promotable Woman #450	$26.95	$22.95		
Sex, Laws & Stereotypes #432	$26.95	$22.95		
Think Like a Manager #451	$26.95	$22.95		
Working Woman's Comm. Survival Guide #5172	$29.95	$22.95		

SPECIAL OFFER:
Orders over $75 receive
FREE SHIPPING

Subtotal	$
Add 7% Sales Tax *(Or add appropriate state and local tax)*	$
Shipping and Handling *($3 one item; 50¢ each additional item)*	$
Total	$
VOLUME DISCOUNTS AVAILABLE — CALL 1-800-258-7248	

Name_____Title_____

Organization _____

Address _____

City _____State/Province _____ZIP/Postal Code _____

Payment choices:
❑ Enclosed is my check/money order payable to National Seminars.
❑ Please charge to: ❑ MasterCard   ❑ VISA   ❑ American Express

Signature X_____Exp. Date _____Card Number _____
❑ Purchase Order #_____

MAIL: Complete and mail order form   **PHONE**:   **FAX**:
    with payment to: Call toll-free **1-800-258-7248**   **1-913-432-0824**
    National Press Publications
    P.O. Box 419107   **INTERNET: http://www.natsem.com/books.html**
    Kansas City, MO 64141-6107